Complete EnglishSmart

Grade 2

Marilyn Kennedy

ISBN : 1-894810-65-1

Copyright © 2004 **Popular Book Company (Canada) Limited**

All rights reserved. No part of this publication may be reproduced, stored in a retrieval system, or transmitted in any form or by any means, electronic, mechanical, photocopying, recording or otherwise, without the prior written permission of the Publisher.

Copies of student pages may be reproduced by the classroom teacher for classroom use only, not for commercial resale. Reproduction of these materials for an entire school or school system is strictly prohibited.

Printed in China

Complete EnglishSmart Contents

Section 1

1. The Bumblebee — 6
- Phonics: Beginning Consonants • Sentence Recognition
- Code Word Game

2. The Museum Trip — 10
- Phonics: Middle and Ending Consonants
- Word Order – Making Sentences • Alike and Different

3. The Eurotunnel — 14
- Phonics: Short Vowels • Subject of a Sentence
- Classification / Grouping

4. Snakes — 18
- Phonics: Long Vowels • Predicate of a Sentence
- Context Clues

5. What Happens Next? — 22
- Phonics: Vowel Digraphs – ai and ay
- Distinguishing Subjects & Predicates • Word Search

6. Days of the Week — 26
- Phonics: Vowel Digraphs – ea and ee
- Telling (Declarative) Sentences • Unscrambling Words

7. The CN Tower — 30
- Phonics: Consonant Blends – bl, cl, fl, gl, pl, and sl
- Asking (Interrogative) Sentences • Identifying Polygons

8. Sir John A. Macdonald — 34
- Phonics: Consonant Blends – br, cr, dr, fr, gr, pr, and tr
- Exclamatory Sentences • Ordinal Numbers

Progress Test 1 — 38

9. Dance Lessons — 44
- Phonics: Consonant Blends – sk, sm, sn, sp, st, and sw
- Imperative (Command) Sentences • Riddles

10. The Treasure Chest — 48
- Phonics: Consonant Digraphs – ch, sh, th, and wh
- Common Nouns • Baby Animals

11. A Visit to the Farm — 52
- Phonics: R-controlled Vowels • Proper Nouns
- Countries and Languages

12. Out on the Town — 56
- Phonics: Dipthongs – ou and ow
- Plural Nouns • Homonyms

13. My Cookbook Recipe – Blueberry Muffins — 60
- Phonics: Special Sounds "oo"
- Verbs (Action Words) • Synonyms

14. The Coin Collection — 64
- Phonics: Dipthongs – oi and oy
- "Being" Verbs (am, is, are) • Antonyms

15. Autumn — 68
- Phonics: "Sad" Sounds – au and aw
- Subject-Verb Agreement
- Synonyms, Homonyms, and Antonyms

16. All about Plants — 72
- Phonics: Words with "y" as a Vowel
- Past Tense Verbs • Months of the Year

17. Penguins — 76
- Phonics: Soft and Hard "g" and "c"
- Irregular Past Tense Verbs • Word Search

Progress Test 2 — 80

Section 2

1. Nouns (1) — 88
- Rhyming Nouns • Noun Word Families
- Categorizing Noun Groups • Identifying / Sorting Nouns

2. Nouns (2) — 92
- Proper Nouns • Common Nouns
- Proper & Common Noun Review

3. Plural Nouns — 96
- Distinguishing between "s" & "es"
- Nouns Ending in "ch" or "sh" • Noun Riddles

4. Pronouns — 100
- Subject & Object Pronouns • Pronoun Review

5. Verbs (1) — 104
- Using Verbs • Naming Verbs
- Recognizing / Identifying Verbs

6. Verbs (2) — 108
- Regular Past Tense Verbs • Irregular Past Tense Verbs
- Linking Verbs (Present Tense)

7. Verbs (3) — 112
- Linking Verbs (Past Tense) • Helping Verbs
- Verb Review

Grade 2

Progress Test 1 — 116

8 — 122
Adjectives
• Adjectives for Size, Shape, Colour, & Number

9 — 126
Articles
• Using "a", "an", & "the" • Parts of Speech Review

10 — 130
Recognizing Sentences
• Sentences & Non-Sentences • Word Order

11 — 134
Sentence Types
• Statements • Questions • Exclamations • Commands

12 — 138
Sentences
• Subjects & Predicates

13 — 142
Punctuation and Capitalization
• Rules of Capitalization • Sentence Beginnings & Endings

14 — 146
Sentence Type Review
• Sentence Types • Subjects & Predicates
• Sentence Beginnings & Endings • Proofreading

Progress Test 2 — 150

Section 3

1 — 158
The Five Senses
• Grouping and Completing Words • Rhyming Words
• Unscrambling Letters to Make Words • Word Search

2 — 162
Changing Seasons
• Grouping Words • Rhyming Words
• Unscrambling Letters to Make Words
• Putting Words in Order to Make Sentences

3 — 166
The Butterfly
• Forming Words • Rhyming Words
• Replacing Pictures with Words • Writing Sentences

4 — 170
Crispy Squares
• Unscrambling Letters to Make Words
• Putting Directions in Correct Order • Writing Sentences

5 — 174
Nunavut
• Completing Sentences
• Unscrambling Letters to Make Words
• Making New Words • Writing Sentences

6 — 178
Word Fun
• Writing an Alphabet Rhyme • A Rhyming Crossword Puzzle
• Homonyms • Acrostic Poetry

7 — 182
What Makes a Fish a Fish?
• Rhyming Words • Correcting Misspelled Words
• Putting Words in Order to Make Sentences
• Writing Sentences

Progress Test 1 — 186

8 — 192
Bat Facts
• Noun Hunt • Rhyming Word Puzzles • Writing Time

9 — 196
The Emperor Penguin
• Word Hunt • Unscrambling Letters to Make Words
• Putting Words in Order to Make Sentences
• Identifying Sentences that Don't Belong

10 — 200
Playing Soccer
• Filling in Speech Bubbles • Describing Words
• Synonyms

11 — 204
Ladybugs
• Rhyming Pairs • Word Meanings • Forming Words
• Putting Words in Order to Make Sentences

12 — 208
The New Umbrella
• Making New Words • Word Search
• Putting Words in Order to Make Sentences
• Identifying Sentences that Don't Belong
• Writing Sentences

13 — 212
Sam the Firefighter
• Completing Words
• Identifying Sentences that Don't Belong
• Homonyms • Writing Sentences about Pictures

14 — 216
The Cactus
• Making Rebus Sentences • Correcting Misspelled Words
• Correcting Words that Don't Make Sense
• Completing Sentences

15 — 220
Marineland
• Putting Words in Order to Make Sentences
• Completing a Crossword Puzzle
• Writing Words Based on Clues

Progress Test 2 — 224

Language Games — 231

Answers — 253

Section 1

Integrated Practice

The Bumblebee

A. Read the story and answer the questions.

The bumblebee is an insect. It is yellow and black and has six legs. Most bumblebees live in a group in a nest. Each group or colony has a queen, worker bees, and drones. The queen is the leader.

The queen bee lays 4 – 8 eggs in the nest after a winter in hibernation. These eggs hatch to become worker bees and drones. The colony grows until it has between 50 – 600 bees. The worker bees help to make new plants grow and they make honey from the nectar in flowering plants.

1. What kind of animal is a bumblebee?
   _____

2. Describe the bumblebee.
   _____

3. Who is the leader of the bumblebee colony?
   _____

4. Where does the queen lay her eggs?
   _____

5. When does the queen lay her eggs?
   _____

6. What is the job of worker bees?
   _____

Phonics: Beginning Consonants

B. The bumblebee is looking for the beehive. Help him find his way. Fill in the missing consonant at the beginning of each word.

1.  __l__ eaf
2.  __p__ ail
3. 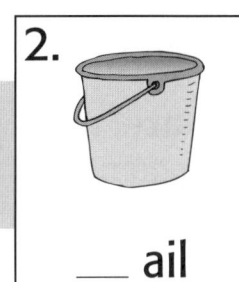 __c__ ap
4. 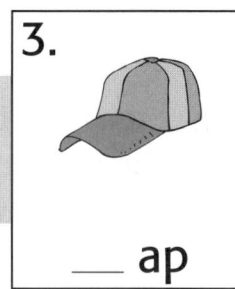 __b__ at

9.  __w__ agon
8.  __g__ oat
7. 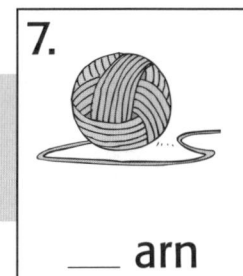 __y__ arn
6.  __j__ ug
5.  __m__ op

10.  __r__ abbit
11.  __d__ rum
12. 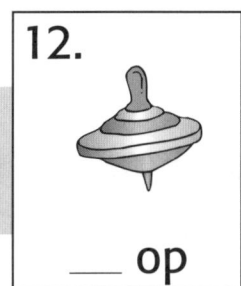 __t__ op
13.  __f__ an
14.  __w__ eb

17. 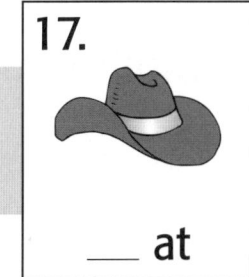 __h__ at
16.  __q__ ueen
15. 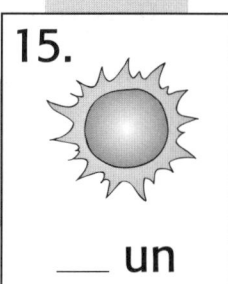 __s__ un

Sentence Recognition

- *A sentence is a group of words that tells about someone or something.*

C. Underline the words that are not sentences. Add the words that you need in order to make them sentences.

1. Polar bears live in the Arctic. They are big and white. Big paws. They have small eyes and ears. Jump from ice floe to ice floe.

   _____

   _____

   _____

2. Polar bears have other names. Sometimes called white bears, sea bears, or ice bears. Swim very well.

   _____

   _____

3. Polar bears move fast and travel far. Eat seals and fish. The male is usually larger than the female. Hairy feet.

   _____

   _____

4. Baby bears or cubs are born in winter. Weigh 2 pounds when born. Remain with mothers from 10 months to 2 years.

   _____

   _____

   _____

Code Word Game

D. Use the code below to read the sentences.

A	B	C	D	E	F	G	H	I	J	K	L	M	N	O
1	2	3	4	5	6	7	8	9	10	11	12	13	14	15

P	Q	R	S	T	U	V	W	X	Y	Z
16	17	18	19	20	21	22	23	24	25	26

1. A square is a shape with four equal sides.

2. A triangle is a shape with three sides.

3. A circle is a single line.

4. A rectangle is a shape with opposite sides that are equal.

2 The Museum Trip

Tomorrow our Grade 2 class is going on a trip to the R.O.M. (Royal Ontario Museum). We will leave school at 9:00 a.m. and return at 3:00 p.m. We have to take our lunch with us.

When we get to the museum, we will visit the Bat Cave, the dinosaurs, and the Egyptian mummies.

The day after our trip, when we get back to school, we will draw pictures and write about what we saw there.

A. Circle ◯ the correct answers.

1. What is the story about?

    A. visiting the school   B. a trip to the museum

    C. looking at dinosaurs

2. What will the children take with them?

    A. snacks   B. lunch   C. a school bag

3. Which of these will they see?

    A. paintings   B. mummies   C. toys

4. What will they do after the trip?

    A. play a game   B. watch a movie   C. draw pictures

Phonics : Middle and Ending Consonants

B. Look at the pictures. Fill in the missing consonant sounds.

1. bu __
2. bo __
3. nes __
4. di __ e
5. tuli __
6. se __ e __
7. mas __
8. ba __
9. po __
10. pe __
11. le __ o __
12. ac __ r __
13. ca __
14. bee __ ive
15. bo __ e
16. bal __
17. sun- __ lower
18. soc __
19. sa __
20. lo __
21. ki __ e
22. ro __ e
23. ra __ e

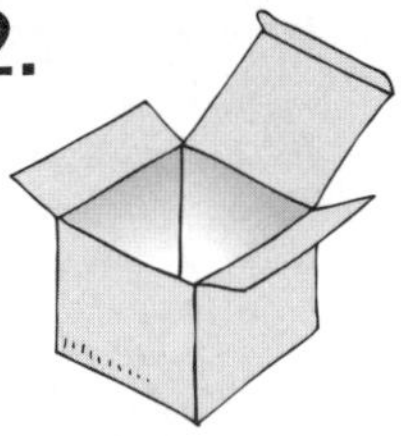

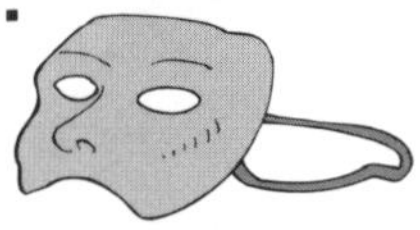

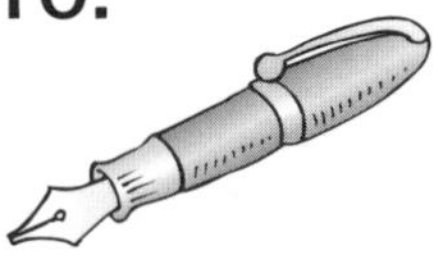

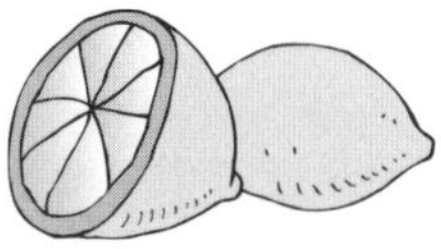

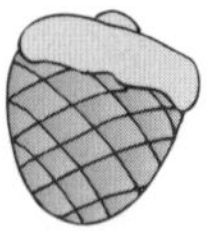

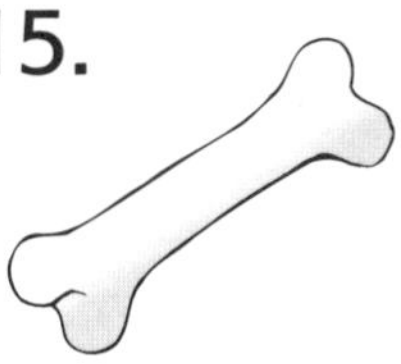

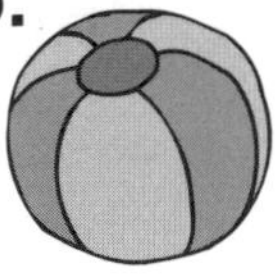

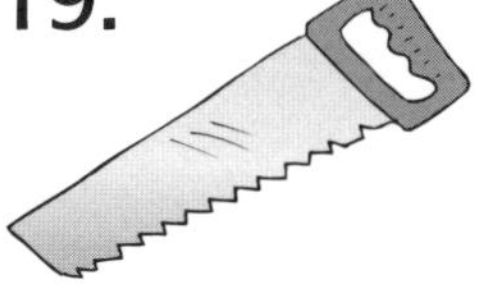

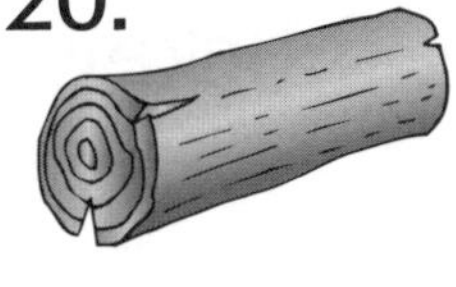

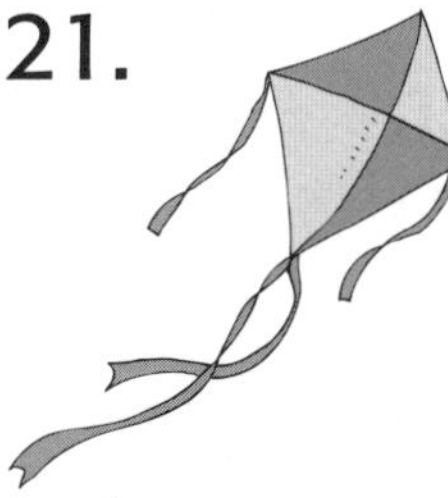

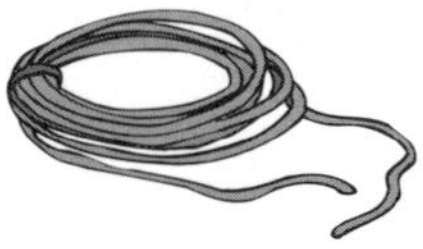

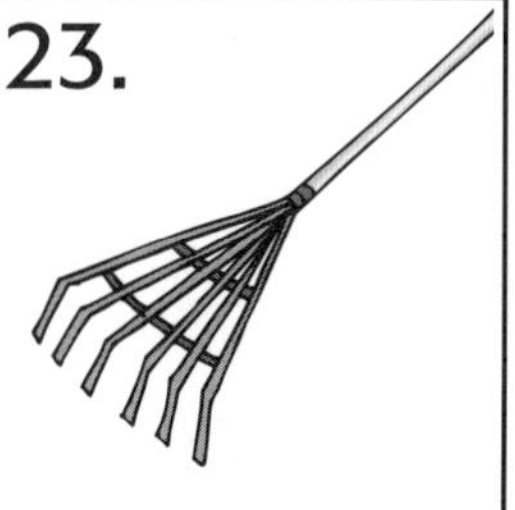

Word Order – Making Sentences

C. Rewrite the following groups of words to make sentences.

1. start autumn. We in school the

_____

2. home. close My is to school

_____

3. to I from day. every walk and school

_____

4. lunch. go I Sometimes, home for

_____

5. sports at There school. of are lots my

_____

6. volleyball. and soccer, play We hockey,

_____

7. floor I games. to like play

_____

Alike and Different

- You can compare things by looking at how they are alike and how they are different. If two things are alike, something about them is the same. If two things are different, something about them is not the same.

D. Look at the pictures. Read the chart. Put a check mark ✔ in the box to indicate the sport being described.

Hockey   **Football**

1. It can be played on ice.
2. It can be played on a field.
3. Something is kicked.
4. There are goalposts.
5. Players run.
6. Players wear skates.
7. Players wear uniforms.
8. Scores are kept.

3 The Eurotunnel

A. Read the letter. Answer the questions.

London, England

Dear Dave,

Guess what? My family is travelling to France this summer. We are driving through the Eurotunnel. Have you ever heard of it? Let me tell you about it.

The idea of a tunnel running under the English Channel is not new. I read that in 1802, an engineer tried to convince the emperor Napoleon to build one. In 1993, it was finally built. Actually, there are really three tunnels: one for trains that carry people one way and another for trains to carry people in the opposite direction. A third service tunnel allows fresh air, repair workers, and emergency vehicles to reach the train tunnels.

I hope you liked hearing about the "Chunnel". I'll write you and tell you all about my trip.

Sincerely,

Rob

1. When was the Eurotunnel built?

2. What body of water does it run through?

3. Why are there three tunnels?

   _____

4. Who is writing the letter?

   _____

 **Phonics: Short Vowels**

B. Rob is looking for the mailbox. Help him find his way. Fill in the missing vowels a, e, i, o, or u.

1. l __ mp
2. w __ b
3. m __ p
4. j __ g
5. p __ t
6. b __ g
7. d __ sk
8. b __ ll
9. n __ t
10. c __ n
11. l __ ps
12. f __ n
13. t __ nt
14. r __ ck
15. s __ x
16. n __ t

Subject of a Sentence

- The subject part of a sentence tells whom or what the sentence is about.

C. Read each sentence. Write a subject for it.

1.  _____ are my favourite fruit.

2.  _____ is the tallest building in North America.

3. 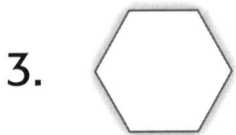 _____ is a figure with six sides.

4.  _____ is 8:15 a.m.

5.  _____ has a monitor and a keyboard.

6.  _____ is my favourite sport.

7.  _____ rotates around the sun.

8.  Draw a picture to match the subject.

   _____ is what I like to do with friends.

Classification / Grouping

D. Louise Ladybug wants to sort some words. Write the words that belong to each group under the first word.

cup   blackboard   Triceratops   desk
Tyrannosaurus   swing   eraser
Stegosaurus   seesaw   pear   bowl
slide   tires   horn
grapes   apple   glass   key

1. plate

2. dinosaur

3. school

4. car

5. playground

6. fruit

Snakes

A. Jake the snake needs help to finish the story. Fill in the missing words for him.

cold   laid   long
eggs   reptiles   hibernation
move   skins   place

Snakes are 1._____ that have 2._____, slender bodies. They have no limbs. They are 3._____ -blooded because they have a low body temperature.

Snakes are non-mammals because they lay 4._____, which hatch soon after they are 5._____. They go into 6._____, or a kind of sleep, for part of the year. Snakes shed their 7._____ several times a year. They 8._____ by slithering from one 9._____ to another.

Phonics: Long Vowels

B. Mike is on a bike ride to the lake. Fill in the blanks with a, i, o, or u.

1.  b __ ke
2. 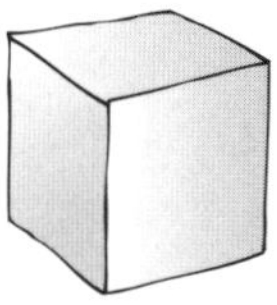 c __ be
3. 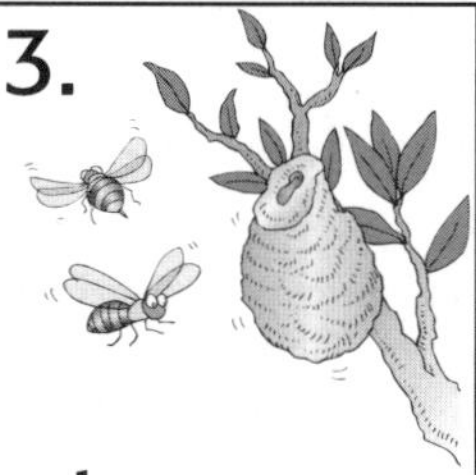 h __ ve
4.  p __ le
5.  c __ ke
6. 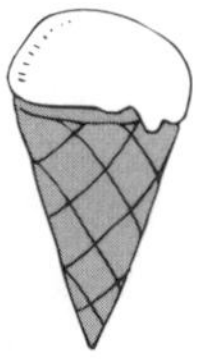 c __ ne
7.  f __ ve
8. 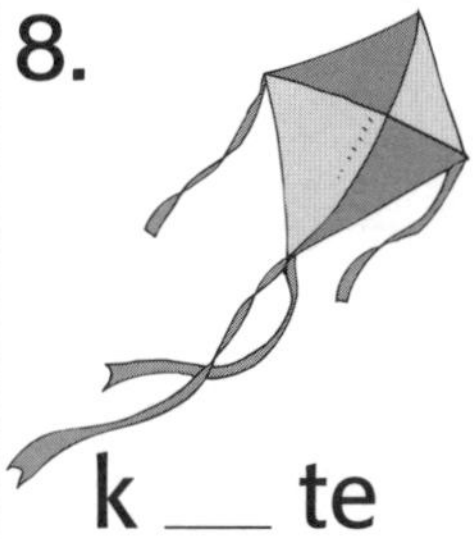 k __ te
9. 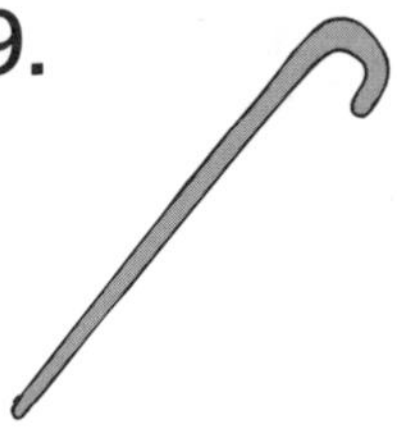 c __ ne
10. 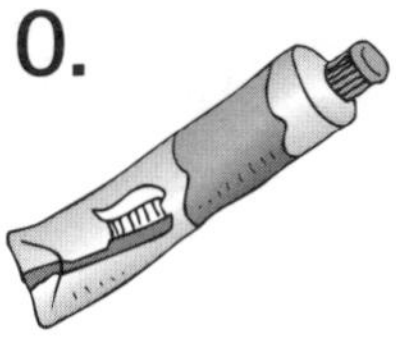 t __ be
11. 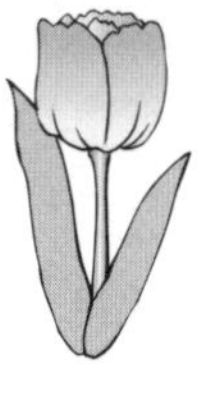 t __ lip
12. 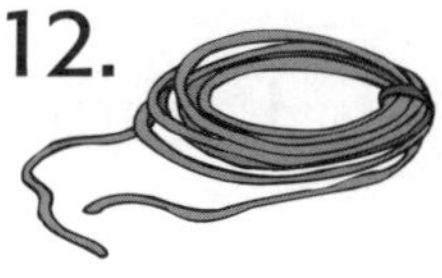 r __ pe
13.  h __ le
14.  g __ te
15. 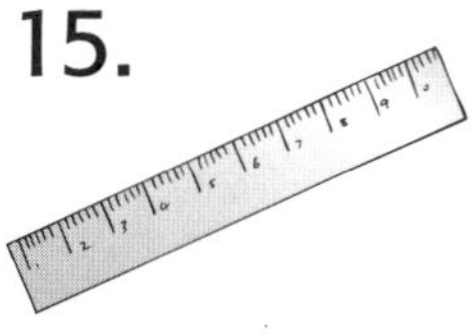 r __ ler
16.  l __ ke

Predicate of a Sentence

- The predicate is the part of the sentence that tells what the subject is doing.

C. Write a predicate for each sentence.

1. In winter, I _____ .

2. In summer, we _____ .

3. In fall, I _____ .

4. In spring, flowers _____ .

5. Ladybugs _____ .

6. My favourite sport _____ .

7. On Valentine's Day, we _____ .

8. The best vacation I ever had _____

    _____ .

9. My secret place _____

    _____ .

10. My family _____

    _____ .

Context Clues

D. Read the story. Use the boldfaced words to fill in the blanks.

Cooking with Mom

Mom and I took out the **recipe** for Rice Krispie Cookies from the recipe **box**. The **ingredients** included rice krispies, marshmallows, and butter. We got the rice krispies and marshmallows from the **cupboard** and the butter from the **refrigerator**.

We heated the butter in a **pot** on the **stove**. When the butter was **melted**, we added the marshmallows. Then we stirred in the rice krispies. Lastly, we scooped the mixture out of the bowl and into a **square** pan.

1. A _____ gives directions for cooking.

2. They are sometimes kept in a _____ .

3. The _____ are the things used in cooking something.

4. Dry ingredients are often kept in a _____ .

5. Butter needs to be stored in a _____ .

6. You can heat something in a _____ on a _____ until it is _____ .

7. Our cookie mixture went into a _____ pan.

What Happens Next?

A. Write what you think will happen next. Give the story to a friend and ask him/her to write his/her ideas below yours.

Jane went out to play. She called on her friend, Sarah, but she wasn't at home. Then she went to Christine's house, but she wasn't at home either. Jane felt sad. There was no one to play with.

Your ideas

Your friend's ideas

Phonics : Vowel Digraphs – ai and ay

B. Find the words with "ai" and "ay" that match the riddles.

play   day   jay   paint   tray   tail   snail   pay   nail   say

1. I carry my house on my back.
   _____

2. I have 24 hours.
   _____

3. I hold things together when you are building.
   _____

4. I am a blue bird.
   _____

5. You can carry things on me.
   _____

6. I make colourful pictures.
   _____

7. I am found at the back of a dog.
   _____

8. You must do this if you want to buy something.
   _____

9. This is what you do when you speak.
   _____

10. You like to do this with your friends.
    _____

Distinguishing Subjects & Predicates

- A sentence has two main parts – a subject and a predicate.
- The subject tells whom or what the sentence is about.
- The predicate tells what is happening.

C. Match the subjects with the predicates. Write the sentences on the lines below.

Subject	Predicate
The monkey	helps clean the cages.
At the zoo, we	has a mane on its neck.
The African elephant	is black and white.
The zebra	likes to hang by its tail.
The male lion	visit the animals.
The tiger	is orange and black.
The zookeeper	is the largest living land animal.

1. _____
2. _____
3. _____
4. _____
5. _____
6. _____
7. _____

Word Search

D. Find the words below in the word search puzzle.

snail   mail   may   fail   crayon   tray   nail
trail   pay   maybe   clay   say   hail   ray   day
play   hay   sail   jay   pray

i	m	g	f	d	l	k	u	b	o	e	h	r	z	j	z
x	q	z	g	x	h	z	m	p	x	m	a	i	l	a	d
a	k	s	w	a	s	q	a	b	c	x	y	g	c	f	s
q	w	f	s	w	h	o	f	x	h	s	w	m	z	l	w
h	b	k	n	e	b	k	r	b	d	e	x	f	h	k	t
r	o	x	a	l	m	n	o	k	o	d	a	h	l	g	r
p	k	f	i	q	a	g	z	l	g	n	q	l	w	z	a
q	g	c	l	a	y	o	c	z	z	z	c	z	s	n	i
r	o	e	q	c	d	k	d	r	d	a	z	n	a	i	l
b	h	q	t	e	l	f	e	s	w	e	h	f	y	j	h
q	x	o	r	v	b	p	r	a	y	r	l	n	m	c	z
z	d	r	a	f	w	f	w	d	n	p	q	l	r	j	d
p	l	a	y	w	o	x	o	r	s	t	i	s	a	o	r
s	t	x	x	h	e	d	x	h	x	a	x	h	r	g	b
g	d	h	b	o	l	k	b	c	h	r	i	m	f	g	g
r	x	o	f	r	b	s	l	e	t	s	g	l	b	j	c
e	f	p	e	c	r	t	n	p	f	h	l	r	k	k	r
o	r	r	p	y	d	o	x	d	y	k	o	d	r	f	a
r	h	z	a	z	z	l	b	a	w	x	k	s	p	a	y
j	x	d	j	y	h	v	j	x	m	a	r	b	a	i	o
s	t	n	h	c	z	e	r	k	d	x	e	r	g	l	n
h	r	m	l	x	m	l	b	x	m	a	y	b	e	r	n

Complete EnglishSmart • Grade 2

6 Days of the Week

Sunday	Monday	Tuesday	Wednesday

A. Benjamin Bunny has a special week ahead. Can you guess what is happening on each day? Finish the sentences.

1. On Sunday, it will be _____

2. On Monday, _____

3. On Tuesday, _____

4. On Wednesday, _____

5. On Thursday, _____

6. On Friday, _____

Draw a picture of something you think Benjamin would like to do on Saturday and complete the sentence.

7. On Saturday, _____

_____

_____

Thursday	Friday	Saturday

Phonics: Vowel Digraphs – ea and ee

B. Underline the correct word that fits each sentence.

1. The (bee, beat) makes its home in a hive.
2. The blue (jeans, beans) are hanging on the line.
3. It's nice to have a cup of (tea, tee).
4. The baseball (teem, team) plays in summer.
5. The (bean, been) plant grew very high.
6. We will have some (meat, meet) for dinner.
7. Mom is going to (weed, week) the garden.
8. There are seven days in a (weak, week).
9. We sail our boat on the (sea, see).
10. This (seed, seek) will grow into a plant.
11. The bird's (beak, bean) is orange.

Telling (Declarative) Sentences

- A telling sentence tells you something. It begins with a capital and ends with a period.

  Example: Bees get nectar from flowers.

C. Colour the picture and write four sentences about what you see.

1. _____

2. _____

3. _____

4. _____

Unscrambling Words

D. Unscramble the words and write them in the correct order on the blank lines. The days of the week and months of the year begin with a capital letter.

ptmeSereb   yaM   udseTay   raaJuny   yJlu   cmbeDeer
erarFbuy   ydaFir   suAutg   sneWdeyda   crhaM
cObreto   shTuyard   nSdyua   vmNeorbe   eJnu   udraStya   odyaMn   lArpi

1. **Days of the Week**

_____   _____
_____   _____
_____   _____
_____   _____

2. **Months of the Year**

_____   _____
_____   _____
_____   _____
_____   _____
_____   _____
_____   _____

The CN Tower

A. Read the story. Finish the sentences.

The CN (Canadian National) Tower in Toronto, Canada is the tallest self-supporting tower in the world. It is as high as five and one-half football fields and has a foundation that is as deep as a five-storey building.

The CN Tower was built to improve the broadcasting of radio and television signals. Many people have used it to break world records, like the person who hopped down its 1,967 steps on a pogo stick.

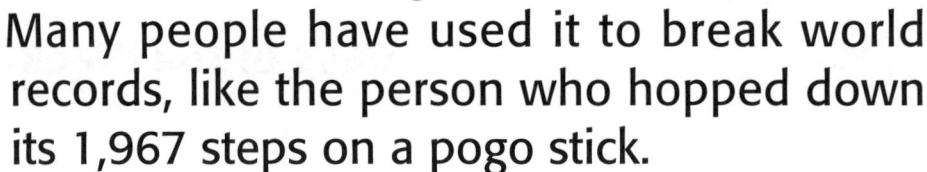

1. The CN Tower is the tallest _____

2. It is as high as _____

3. Its foundation is _____

4. The CN Tower was built to _____

5. One of the world records at the CN Tower was

Phonics : Consonant Blends – bl, cl, fl, gl, pl, and sl

B. Write the missing consonant blends in the blanks. Use the letters in the flowers.

1. Robert picked _____ owers from the garden.

2. Michael saw the _____ owns at the circus.

3. The children played on the _____ ide.

4. Kathleen went to _____ eep early.

5. The _____ ass broke into many pieces.

6. They took the _____ ed out in the winter.

7. There is a Canadian _____ ag in front of our school.

8. Clare _____ ew out the candles on the cake.

9. Maggie put the cookies on the _____ ate.

10. They were _____ ad they took their time.

11. The _____ ock in the hall struck midnight.

12. At recess, we _____ ay outside.

Asking (Interrogative) Sentences

- An asking sentence asks a question.
- It begins with a capital and ends with a question mark (?).

  Example: What does your spaceship look like?

C. **Albert the alien has just landed his spaceship on Earth. If you could ask him five questions, what would they be?**

1. _____

2. _____

3. _____

4. _____

5. _____

Ask a friend to pretend that he or she is Albert and answer your questions.

Identifying Polygons

A polygon is a shape with 3 or more sides.

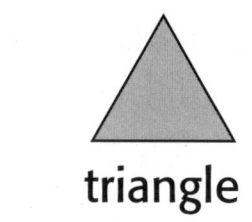
triangle

quadrilateral

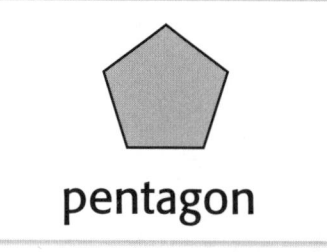
pentagon

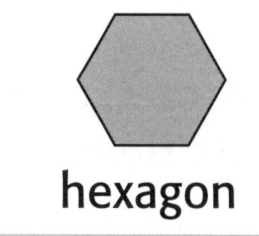
hexagon

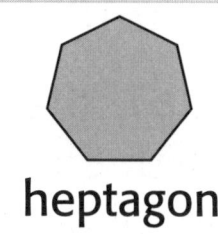
heptagon

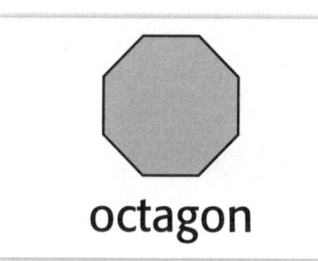
octagon

D. For each case, draw the shape that matches the description.

1. polygon with 3 sides

2. polygon with 4 sides

3. polygon with 5 sides

4. polygon with 6 sides

5. polygon with 7 sides

6. polygon with 8 sides

8 Sir John A. Macdonald

A. Read the story and answer the questions.

The first prime minister of Canada was Sir John A. Macdonald. He was born in Glasgow, Scotland and came to Kingston, Ontario in 1816 at the age of five. He became a lawyer in 1836.

In 1867, the Dominion of Canada was formed with Sir John A. as its head. He was best known for his part in the completion of the Pacific Railway. He died in 1881 in Ottawa, the nation's capital.

1. Who was the first prime minister of Canada?

   _____

2. Where was he born?

   _____

3. How old was he when he came to Ontario?

   _____

4. What year was the Dominion of Canada formed?

   _____

5. What was Sir John A. best known for?

   _____

6. Where did he die?

   _____

Phonics : Consonant Blends – br, cr, dr, fr, gr, pr, and tr

B. Choose the consonant blends on the bricks below to fill in the blanks and build the tower.

| br | cr | dr | fr | gr | pr | tr |

1. _____ une
2. _____ ime
3. _____ op
4. _____ ip
5. _____ ape
6. _____ ing
7. _____ eam
8. _____ uit
9. _____ aid
10. _____ ass
11. _____ ass
12. _____ ize
13. _____ ee
14. _____ ee
15. _____ og
16. _____ um
17. _____ ess
18. _____ uck
19. _____ ab
20. _____ eed
21. _____ eed
22. _____ eed
23. _____ eed
24. _____ ame
25. _____ een
26. _____ one
27. _____ ime
28. _____ ime
29. _____ ap
30. _____ ail
31. _____ ue
32. _____ oom

Exclamatory Sentences

- Wow! An exclamatory sentence is a sentence that shows strong feeling.
- It begins with a capital letter and ends with an exclamation mark (!).

C. Look at the pictures and read the sentences. Write exclamations to match.

1.  You learned to ride a two-wheeler.

   _____

2. You won 1st prize.

   _____

3. You have a new puppy.

   _____

4. You have just read your first book.

   _____

5.  You just learned to swim.

   _____

6. You found a $10 bill on the ground.

   _____

7.  You are going to Disney World.

   _____

Ordinal Numbers

- *Ordinals are words that state the order of people or things.*

D. Look at the pictures and their ordinals. Complete the sentences below.

first

second

third

fourth

fifth

sixth

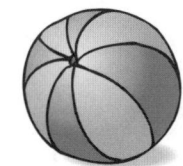
seventh

eighth

ninth

tenth

1. The basketball is _____ .
2. The ping pong ball is _____ .
3. The baseball is _____ .
4. The tennis ball is _____ .
5. The hockey puck is _____ .
6. The beachball is _____ .
7. The shuttlecock is _____ .
8. The football is _____ .
9. The volleyball is _____ .
10. The golf ball is _____ .

PROGRESS TEST 1

Word Families

A. Read the word at the beinning of each group. Read the sentences. Fill in the words that make sense.

Change one letter.

1. **road**
   - They drove down the _____ .
   - The _____ and the frog are friends.
   - He lifted the _____ of bricks.

2. **like**
   - I _____ to eat at McDonald's.
   - Mary rode her _____ to the store.
   - Dad and I went for a _____ .
   - A _____ is a kind of fish.

3. **game**
   - We played a _____ of chess.
   - She _____ to my birthday party.
   - The baby lion is very _____ .
   - Her _____ is Judy.

4. **bake**
   - She will _____ some cookies for us.
   - Will you _____ your umbrella today?
   - The _____ tastes delicious.
   - The _____ is clear and blue.
   - Mom told David to _____ the lawn.

5. day
- It is a beautiful _____ .
- The _____ is a type of bird.
- The first _____ of sunshine beat down.
- Did she _____ where she was going?
- They found their _____ home.
- Her birthday is in the month of _____ .

Beginning, Middle, and Ending Consonants

B. Fill in the missing consonants.

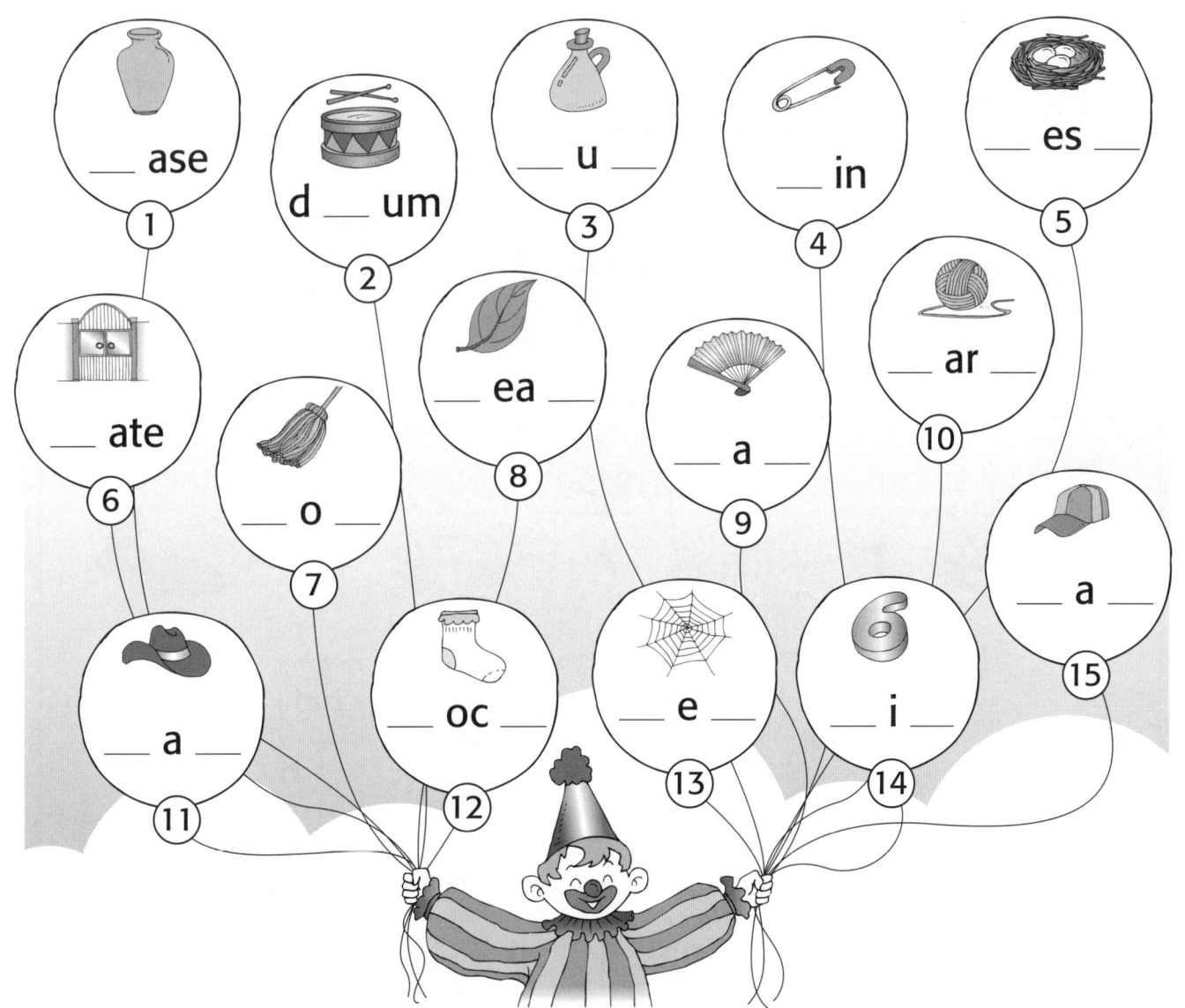

Short and Long Vowels

C. David loves baseball. Help him reach home base by filling in the missing vowels.

The Baseball Game

11. f __ ve
10. r __ ke
9. c __ be
12. h __ nd
1. t __ be
8. f __ sh
2. c __ ke
7. t __ nt
3. l __ g
4. b __ ne
5. p __ le
6. h __ ve

Vowel Digraphs and Consonant Blends

D. Find the words listed below in the word search.

flag   tray   blue   reed   fruit   pail   tail
slide   weed   cream   play   plate   been
dream   tree   glass   clock   bean
week   prize   grass   broom

y	l	w	g	w	t	r	a	y	q	x	p	z	p	z	s
x	w	e	k	x	a	h	i	x	p	d	w	f	e	k	d
f	h	h	i	c	i	x	t	a	b	k	o	p	r	i	b
l	t	p	a	i	l	k	e	f	c	x	c	l	o	c	k
a	w	l	o	z	s	i	v	r	i	u	o	a	v	d	c
g	l	a	s	s	f	h	t	o	d	s	r	t	f	m	i
z	t	y	m	o	a	d	u	w	b	l	u	e	m	i	x
p	y	x	s	t	n	o	j	m	e	i	n	f	c	k	b
b	a	t	w	e	s	n	r	o	e	d	e	j	n	b	r
i	w	o	o	r	x	b	e	a	n	e	k	a	i	a	o
s	c	w	f	x	i	c	e	q	x	j	q	u	w	q	o
x	j	s	p	w	e	e	d	y	u	w	y	w	e	u	m
a	b	z	i	e	h	l	k	o	i	a	f	h	q	a	c
v	l	d	r	e	a	m	s	r	x	l	r	l	c	b	o
e	v	s	w	k	t	h	t	s	h	v	u	t	r	e	e
w	h	z	d	w	c	x	j	b	p	r	i	z	e	x	g
o	j	o	w	g	p	e	z	i	g	x	t	g	a	g	o
g	r	a	s	s	x	v	h	q	c	o	s	z	m	d	x

Sentences

E. Read the sentences. Give each one a correct ending and circle "T" for telling, "A" for asking, and "E" for exclamatory.

1. Kathleen loves chocolate cake	T	A	E
2. Will David take out the garbage	T	A	E
3. They shop at the mall	T	A	E
4. I won the first prize	T	A	E
5. Do you like ice cream	T	A	E
6. Oh no	T	A	E

F. Underline the nouns and circle the verbs.

1. The car drove down the highway.
2. The bird laid the eggs in the nest.
3. Mom bakes great cakes at home.
4. Tom walks to school every day.
5. She likes to take the dog for a walk.

G. For each sentence, fill in a subject and a predicate.

1. The _____ _____ to the beach.
2. An _____ _____ a fruit.
3. Many _____ _____ to the farm daily.

4. Every _____ , we _____ to the lunchroom.
5. Each _____ , they _____ skiing.
6. A _____ _____ a vehicle.

Subject / Predicate Match-up

H. Read the subject parts of the sentences. Match them with the predicate parts by writing the letters in the boxes.

The subject tells whom or what the sentence is about. The predicate tells what the subject is doing.

1. The clown	B	A.	came down from the sky.
2. The police officer		B.	wore face make-up.
3. A train		C.	arrested the thief.
4. Five frogs		D.	are beautiful birds.
5. Dad		E.	chugged along the tracks.
6. My school		F.	jumped on the lily pad.
7. Trees		G.	broke down near the house.
8. A comet		H.	gave me a big hug.
9. Blue jays		I.	has a big gymnasium.
10. The car		J.	often turn colours in Autumn.

9 Dance Lessons

A. Read the story. Choose the words that fit in the blanks. Circle ◯ the answers of the questions below.

> dance   three   ten   jive   fun   good   day
> eighteen   ballet   dances   many
> slippers   ballet   costumes

When Kathleen was ¹._____ years old, she started to learn ²._____ . She wore a pink leotard and tiny ballet ³._____ . She practised the steps every ⁴._____ .

By the time she was ⁵._____ years old, she was very good at ⁶._____ . She learned ⁷._____ new steps and routines. In no time at all, she was very ⁸._____ at jazz, too!

Later, when Kathleen was ⁹._____ , she saw a ¹⁰._____ competition on television. She liked the ¹¹._____ and the ¹²._____ , too. The people were the same age as she and they were having ¹³._____ .

Now, Kathleen is learning the ¹⁴._____ .

15. What is the main topic?

    A. dance lessons   B. dance routines   C. dancing shoes

16. How old was Kathleen when she learned jazz?

    A. eighteen   B. ten   C. three

Phonics: Consonant Blends – sk, sm, sn, sp, st, and sw

B. Write the correct word for each sentence. Use the words in the box.

> snake   skunk   stove   spoon   snack
> small   skate   stairs   smells   steps
> space   swim   skip   swat   snip   snap

1. Yum! That meat really _____ good!

2. There are many galaxies in outer _____ .

3. There are two sets of _____ in our house.

4. Mom cooked dinner on the _____ .

5. The _____ slithered in the grass.

6. Oh no! There's a _____ by the tree.

7. What is your _____ for recess?

8. We will go for a _____ .

9. She can _____ with a rope.

10. The _____ child was shy.

11. Kathleen tried to _____ the fly.

12. She tried to _____ the thread with the scissor.

13. Can you _____ your fingers?

14. I set the table with a fork, a knife, and a _____ .

Imperative (Command) Sentences

- A command is a sentence that tells someone to do something.

C. **Robert is teaching his dog, Punkie, to obey commands. Unscramble the words to read the commands.**

1. bone , the Punkie . Fetch
   _____
   _____

2. newspaper . and Punkie , get the go
   _____
   _____

3. shoe . Find Punkie , the
   _____
   _____

4. mouth . leash Take in the your
   _____
   _____

5. toy . the Find
   _____
   _____

6. chase Don't the car .
   _____
   _____

Riddles

D. Use the words and pictures to help you solve the riddles below.

Toonies, Loonies, and Such

penny	nickel	dime	quarter	loonie	toonie

1. I am worth 1¢.
   I am smaller than a nickel but bigger than a dime.
   I have maple leaves.

   _____

2. I am worth $2.00.
   I am silver and gold.
   I am the largest coin.

   _____

3. I am worth 10¢.
   I am the smallest coin.
   I have a schooner called the Bluenose.

   _____

4. I am worth 25¢.
   I am larger than a nickel but smaller than a loonie.
   I have a caribou.

   _____

5. I am worth $1.00.
   I am golden.
   I have a loon on the front.

   _____

6. I am worth 5¢.
   I am silver.
   I am larger than a dime but smaller than a quarter.

   _____

10 The Treasure Chest

Dear David,

Guess what! We went to Sharaz last Thursday. When we arrived, we heard about a sunken ship in the Shallow Sea. The story goes that long ago, a pirate ship sank there and there are still treasure chests aboard it.

We decided to search for the sunken treasure. First, we boarded a small boat and rowed out to the ship. Then, we put on wetsuits and masks and dived under the water.

When we reached the ship, we swam inside and, what do you think? We found a giant chest filled with gold and jewels!

I'll write you as soon as I get home.

Your friend,
Rob

A. Read the letter and answer the questions.

1. What is the main idea of the first paragraph?

   _____
   _____

2. What is the main idea of the second paragraph?

   _____
   _____

3. What is the main idea of the third paragraph?

   _____

   _____

Phonics: Consonant Digraphs – ch, sh, th, and wh

Tongue twisters with ch, sh, th, and wh are sometimes hard to say.

B. Fill in the missing letters to make the tongue twisters.

Sh 1. ____ e sells sea ____ ells by the sea ____ ore.

Ch 2. ____ ester ____ ewed the ____ ewing gum ____ eerily.

Th 3. ____ addeus ____ ought ____ e ____ imble was ____ ick.

Wh 4. Willy the ____ ale ____ irled ____ ile the ____ eel of the ____ ite ____ aler ____ istled.

C. For each case, choose the word that fits.

1. A cat's _____ help her find her way. (whisper, whiskers)

2. This gravy is _____ . (thick, think)

3. The _____ sank in the sea. (ship, shop)

4. The treasure _____ was filled with jewels. (cheat, chest)

5. A _____ is a delicious fruit. (beach, peach)

6. A _____ flies towards light. (moth, math)

Common Nouns

- A common noun names any person, place, or thing.
- It can be singular (one) or plural (more than one).

D. Match the singular nouns with their plural forms.

Singular	Plural	Singular	Plural
1. bat	A. ships	14. hat	N. glasses
2. fox	B. mats	15. road	O. trees
3. plant	C. toys	16. cap	P. tables
4. ship	D. pens	17. rug	Q. girls
5. toy	E. foxes	18. boat	R. pencils
6. flower	F. bats	19. book	S. hats
7. acorn	G. desks	20. glass	T. boys
8. mat	H. cats	21. table	U. caps
9. pen	I. rulers	22. pencil	V. books
10. dog	J. flowers	23. lake	W. roads
11. cat	K. plants	24. tree	X. boats
12. desk	L. dogs	25. girl	Y. rugs
13. ruler	M. acorns	26. boy	Z. lakes

Baby Animals

E. Read the sentences. Look at the pictures and fill in the blanks.

> deer   dog   horse   goose   cat   pig   chicken
> rabbit   cow   kangaroo

1. A foal is a baby _____ .

2. A calf is a baby _____ .

3. A leveret is a baby _____ .

4. A puppy is a baby _____ .

5. A joey is a baby _____ .

6. A piglet is a baby _____ .

7. A chick is a baby _____ .

8. A gosling is a baby _____ .

9. A kitten is a baby _____ .

10. A fawn is a baby _____ .

11 A Visit to the Farm

A. Use the code to fill in the missing blanks. Answer the questions.

A	B	C	D	E	F	G	H	I	J	K	L	M	N	O	P	Q	R	S	T	U	V	W	X	Y	Z
1	2	3	4	5	6	7	8	9	10	11	12	13	14	15	16	17	18	19	20	21	22	23	24	25	26

There are **MANY** different kinds of **FARMS**. Some are **DAIRY** farms and some are **CATTLE** farms. There are others that grow **VEGETABLES**, like **CORN**, **POTATOES**, and **CARROTS**. In the West, farmers grow **WHEAT**.

We **VISITED** a farm with our **CLASS**. It was a **DAIRY** farm, so the animals were all **COWS**. The farmer **SHOWED** us how the cows are **MILKED** using big machines.

We had lots of **FUN** at the **FARM**.

1. What is the main idea of the story?

_____

2. What kind of farm did the children visit?

_____

Phonics: R-controlled Vowels

- When the letter "r" follows a vowel, it changes the sound of the vowel.

B. Arnie the farmer is going to the market. Help him get there. Underline the correct words.

Arnie's (form, farm) is (for, far) from the (market, marked). Every day, Arnie (works, worms) very (hard, harm). He (turms, turns) the soil, which is sometimes called (dirt, diet). When there are lots of (warms, worms) in the soil, it is healthy. There are also lots of animals on the (form, farm). Some are (horns, horses) and others are pigs, from which Arnie gets (park, pork) to sell at the market.

Proper Nouns

- A proper noun names a specific person, place, or thing.
- It always begins with a capital.

C. Colour the sides of the books that contain proper nouns.

1.
boy | Mark

2.
Ottawa | city

3.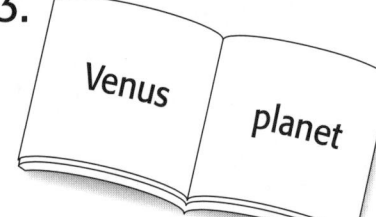
Venus | planet

4.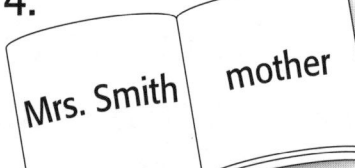
Mrs. Smith | mother

5.
Sun | star

6.
dog | Punkie

7.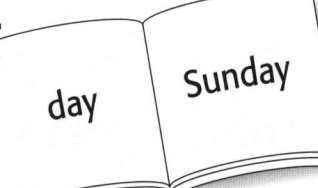
Portland Drive | street

8.
Mars | chocolate bar

9.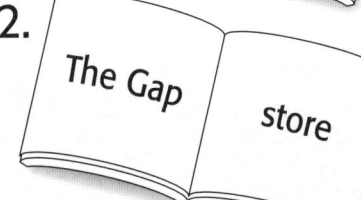
Canada Day | holiday

10.
day | Sunday

11.
Deer Lake | town

12.
The Gap | store

13.
Charlotte's Web | book

14.
month | May

15.
Humber | river

16.
Air Canada | airline

17.
Park Street School | school

Countries and Languages

D. Read the chart. Use it to fill in the blanks.

Country	Language
Spain	Spanish
Italy	Italian
France	French
Greece	Greek
Canada	English
Romania	Romanian
Hungary	Hungarian

Many countries in the world have people who speak 1._____ , such as Canada. In Spain, people speak 2._____ and in 3._____ , people speak French. In the Eastern European countries of Hungary and Romania, people speak 4._____ and 5._____ . Italy and Greece, in the Mediterranean, have people who speak 6._____ and 7._____ .

E. Unscramble these languages.

1. LIAANTI	2. HASPNSI	3. GRHUAIANN
_____	_____	_____

Out on the Town

A. Carly Cow has escaped from the farm! She's out on the town. Help her find her way home. Match the story titles below with the pictures in the maze. Print the letters in the boxes.

A. Time to Nibble
B. Home Sweet Home
C. Time for a Drink
D. Carly Turns the Curve
E. On the Straight and Narrow
F. Carly Hits the Fence

Phonics : Dipthongs – ou and ow

- Dipthongs are two vowels that make a new sound.

B. Say the words in the clouds below and print them where they belong.

hound   grow   blow   row   blouse

couch   glow   town   brown   rainbow

mouse   low   flowers   crown   sound

cl<u>ow</u>n	h<u>ou</u>se	sn<u>ow</u>man

Plural Nouns

C. Look at the picture. Find the objects listed below. Count them and write the plural nouns.

1. street light — 6 street lights
2. car
3. flower
4. boy
5. bicycle
6. tree
7. parking meter
8. truck

Homonyms

- Homonyms are word pairs that sound the same but have different meanings and are spelled differently.

D. Match the pictures and words on the left side of the page with the homonyms on the right.

1.  pear ☐ A. sea

2. 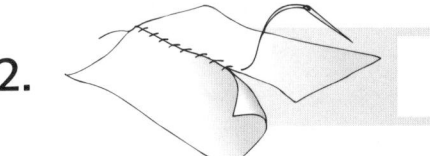 sew ☐ B. blew

3.  blue ☐ C. tow

4. 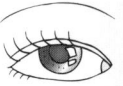 see ☐ D. so

5. 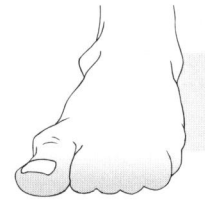 toe ☐ E. pair

13 My Cookbook Recipe – Blueberry Muffins

A. Read the cookbook recipe below. Circle ◯ the correct answers.

1. Turn the oven up to 400° F.
2. Get these ingredients together.
   2 cups of flour
   1/2 cup of sugar
   1/2 cup of margarine (melted)
   1/2 tsp. of salt
   3 tsp. of baking powder
   1 cup of blueberries
   1 egg
   3/4 cup of milk
3. Put all the dry ingredients in a bowl.
4. Put all the wet ingredients in a bowl.
5. Mix the dry ingredients with the wet ingredients.
6. Spoon the mixture into a muffin pan.
7. Bake at 400° F for 15 – 20 minutes.

1. This recipe is for (muffins, cookies).

2. Milk is a (wet, dry) ingredient.

3. The fruit in this recipe is (blackberries, blueberries).

4. The seventh ingredient is (egg, milk).

5. The oven is turned up to (400°F, 400°C).

Phonics: Special Sounds "oo"

- Words that have "oo" in them can sound like "oo" in "room" or "oo" in "cook".

B. Find the words that are missing from the word banks in the diagrams.

The Cookbook

My mom taught me to 1._____

By reading a 2._____ .

She said, " Take a 3._____ .

This is called a 4._____ ."

Word bank: cookbook, book, cook, look

The Clown

The clown played the 5._____

Jumping in the 6._____ .

He thought it was 7._____

When he started to 8._____ .

Word bank: drool, pool, fool, cool

Verbs (Action Words)

- Verbs are words that describe actions.

  Example: running – She is running a race.

C. **Find these actions in the picture and write a sentence using each one.**

| swinging | playing | running | climbing | sliding |

1. _____
2. _____
3. _____
4. _____
5. _____

Synonyms

- Synonyms are words that mean the same thing.

D. Read each sentence below. Look at the picture. Circle ◯ the word that matches the one underlined.

	1. Mark was <u>weeping</u> when he fell down. crying climbing
2. It was a <u>windy</u> day in the city. breezy cool	
	3. Mom was <u>exhausted</u> after her trip. tired trying
4. The <u>small</u> child held on to the balloon. little large	
	5. The weather was <u>humid</u> and warm. damp dry
6. The <u>huge</u> dog ran over to the car. big tiny	
	7. The kiwi fruit were <u>firm</u> and green. hard soft
8. The bike tires were <u>grimy</u> after they went through the mud. dirty wet	

14 The Coin Collection

A. Read the story. Finish the sentences.

David has a coin collection. He started it when he was six years old. He has over three hundred coins in his collection.

The first coins he got were three coins from Italy that his mom gave him after a trip there. Since then, many of his family members and friends have given him gifts of coins. He has coins from all over the world.

David's favourite coin is one from Sri Lanka. It is large and heavy. Another coin he likes is a Chinese one with a hole in the centre.

1. David has a _____
2. He has over _____
3. His first coins were _____
4. Many people have given _____
5. He has coins from _____
6. David's favourite _____
7. His favourite coin is _____
8. A Chinese coin has _____

Phonics : Dipthongs – oi and oy

- "oi" and "oy" sound the same in words, but "oi" is usually found in the middle of a word and "oy" is usually found at the end.

B. Read the sentences below. Fill in the blanks with words from the word bank.

coin   toy   annoy   soy   oil
boy   joy   boil   point   loyal

1. Christine has a _____ collection.

2. The _____ likes to play soccer.

3. Ryan gets a lot of _____ from playing sports.

4. The pencil has a very sharp _____ .

5. Some babies drink _____ milk.

6. Don't _____ your brother!

7. Will you _____ the water for tea?

8. The Game Boy is his favourite _____ .

9. _____ is lighter than water.

10. Marie is a very _____ friend.

"Being" Verbs (am, is, are)

- "Am", "is", and "are" are special verbs that tell about someone or something.

  Rules: Use "am" with "I".

  Use "is" when it's one person, place, or thing.

  Use "are" when it's more than one person, place, or thing.

C. Fill "am", "is", or "are" in the blanks.

1. There _____ three boys in the play.

2. I _____ going to the show with my dad.

3. She _____ planning to see the circus.

4. Maria _____ running to the bus.

5. Kathleen and David _____ cooking a meal.

6. They _____ best friends.

7. We _____ looking for the soccer ball.

8. I _____ riding my bike.

9. Rob _____ driving his car.

10. It _____ a nice morning.

Antonyms

- Antonyms are words with opposite meanings.

D. Read the word inside each heart. Choose the correct antonym from the two words below it.

1.

hot

warm, cold

2.

tall

short, high

3.

fat

heavy, thin

4.

dry

heat, wet

5.

happy

funny, sad

6.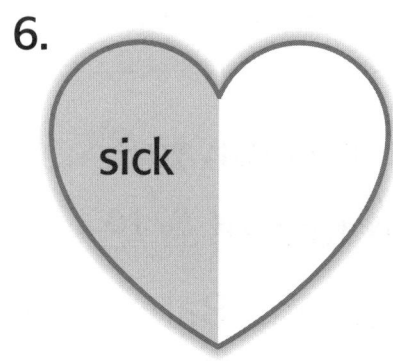

sick

healthy, ill

7.

black

green, white

8.

afraid

brave, scared

9.

ask

question, answer

15 Autumn

A. Read the words below. Find the spaces where they belong in the story.

carpet   beautiful   season   fall   fawn
Summer   woods   because   colour   hike
animals   woods   ground

Autumn is the 1._____ that follows 2._____ . Sometimes, we call it 3._____ . It is very 4._____ 5._____ the leaves change 6._____ and fall to the 7._____ . When they fall, the ground looks like a 8._____ .

It is fun to 9._____ in the Autumn. Often, there are lots of 10._____ in the 11._____ in the Autumn. Baby deer or 12._____ can be seen even in 13._____ near cities.

B. Answer the questions on the lines below.

1. What season follows Summer?

   _____

2. What happens to leaves in the Autumn?

   _____

3. Where do you find baby deer in the Autumn?

   _____

4. What is another name for Autumn?

   _____

5. What season comes after Autumn?

   _____

Phonics: "Sad" Sounds – au and aw

- Both "au" and "aw" make the same sound. When you say "saw" or "pause" out loud, you can hear why these are sad sounds.

Who wants to be a great student?

C. Answer the questions with the correct words from the box. Give yourself the points in the circles. Then, add up your score.

> jaw   Autumn   yawn   auto
> fawn   straw   saw   saucer

1. What is a baby deer? _____ ◯
2. What do you put in a drink? _____ ◯
3. What season is also called "fall"? _____ ◯
4. What can be used to cut wood? _____ ◯
5. What do you do when you are sleepy? _____ ◯
6. What goes on the bottom of a cup? _____ ◯
7. What is another word for car? _____ ◯
8. What is part of your face? _____ ◯

TOTAL: ◯

Subject-Verb Agreement

- The subject of a sentence must have a verb that "agrees".

D. Read the story about beavers. For each case, choose the verb that agrees with the subject of the sentence.

1. Beavers _____ members of the aquatic rodent family. is are

2. Beavers _____ dams of sticks and mud. build builds

3. Every beaver _____ a coat of thick coarse fur. have has

4. Beavers _____ to build their dams in streams and small rivers. likes like

5. Beavers _____ in colonies, with one or more groups to a lodge. live lives

6. A family of beavers _____ of a mother, father, and two sets of offspring. consist consists

7. They _____ in the winter, when two or more kids are born. breed   breeds

8. When they see danger, beavers _____ others by slapping their tails. warn   warns

Synonyms, Homonyms, and Antonyms

E. Read the pair of words in each leaf. Decide if they are synonyms (S), homonyms (H), or antonyms (A). Circle ◯ the correct letter.

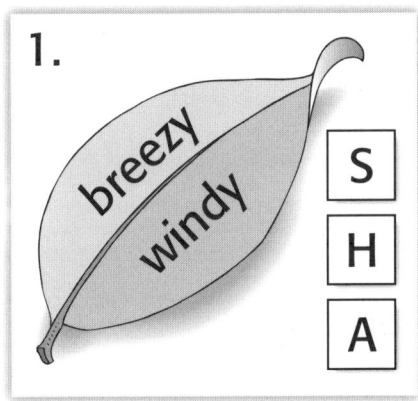
1. breezy / windy — S H A

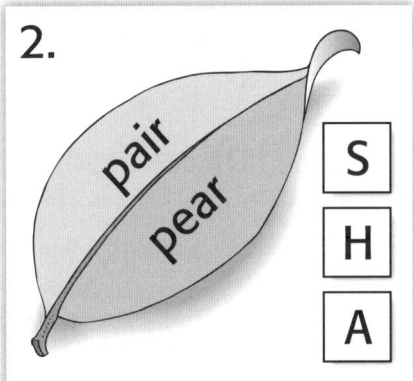
2. pair / pear — S H A

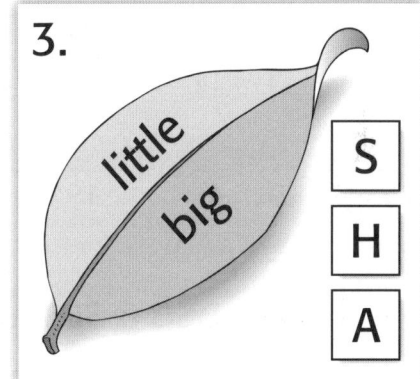
3. little / big — S H A

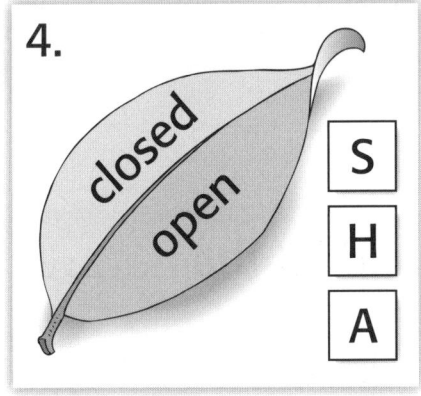
4. closed / open — S H A

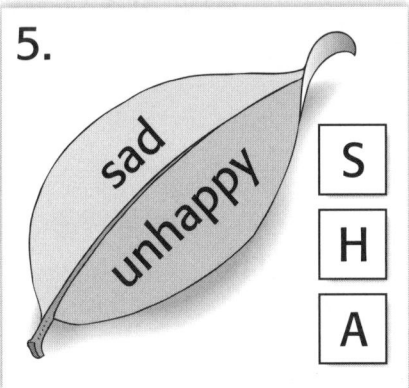
5. sad / unhappy — S H A

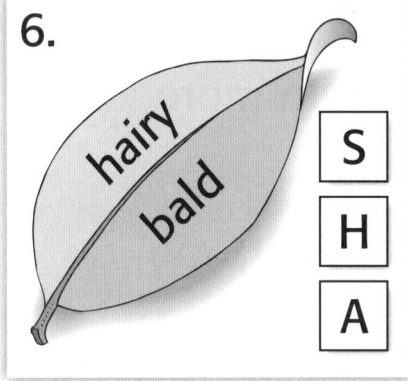
6. hairy / bald — S H A

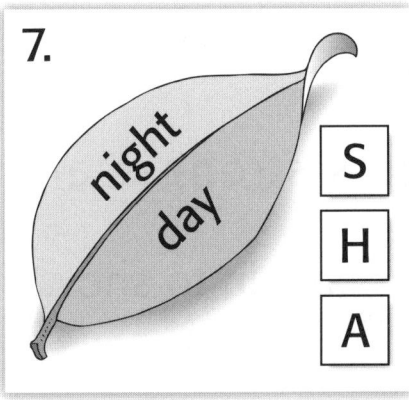
7. night / day — S H A

8. clean / dirty — S H A

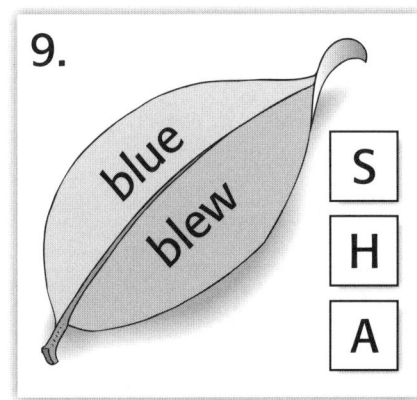
9. blue / blew — S H A

16 All about Plants

A. This is about growing things. Use the code and fill the correct letters in the blanks.

A	B	C	D	E	F	G	H	I	J	K	L	M	N	O	P	Q	R	S	T	U	V	W	X	Y	Z
1	2	3	4	5	6	7	8	9	10	11	12	13	14	15	16	17	18	19	20	21	22	23	24	25	26

Most __ __ __ __ __ __ start as a __ __ __ __ . Usually, you
     16 12 1 14 20 19   19 5 5 4

__ __ __ __ __ the __ __ __ __ in the __ __ __ __ __ __ of the
16 12 1 14 20   19 5 5 4   7 1 18 4 5 14

__ __ __ __ , in __ __ __ __ __ or __ __ __ .
25 1 18 4   19 8 1 4 5   19 21 14

If you use a small __ __ __ __ __ __ , you can dig a __ __ __ __
                20 18 15 23 5 12   8 15 12 5

just big enough to __ __ __ __ the seed down and __ __ __ __ __
               16 15 11 5   3 15 22 5 18

it with more __ __ __ __ .
          19 15 9 12

First, you __ __ __ __ __ the __ __ __ __ and let the __ __ __
         16 12 1 14 20   19 5 5 4   19 21 14

shine down on it. After a few __ __ __ __ __ , little shoots begin
                          23 5 5 11 19

to __ __ __ __ __ __ . Then, the
   19 16 18 15 21 20

__ __ __ __ gets stronger and
19 20 5 13

__ __ __ __ __ __ begin to show.
12 5 1 22 5 19

Phonics: Words with "y" as a Vowel

- Sometimes when "y" is at the end of a word, it sounds like an "e".
  Examples: many, only, bunny

B. Say the words on the left. Match them with the meanings.

funny	•	•	another name for rabbit
honey	•	•	causing laughter
money	•	•	bright with sunshine
Mary	•	•	a sweet, sticky fluid made by bees
bunny	•	•	a name for a girl
sunny	•	•	used for buying and selling things

Sometimes, the "y" at the end of a word sounds like an "i".

C. Fill in the missing words.

my   try   Why   fly   shy

1. _____ did she go to the store?
2. Did you _____ to ride the bike?
3. We can _____ our kites another day.
4. The child was very _____ .
5. We can go to _____ house to play.

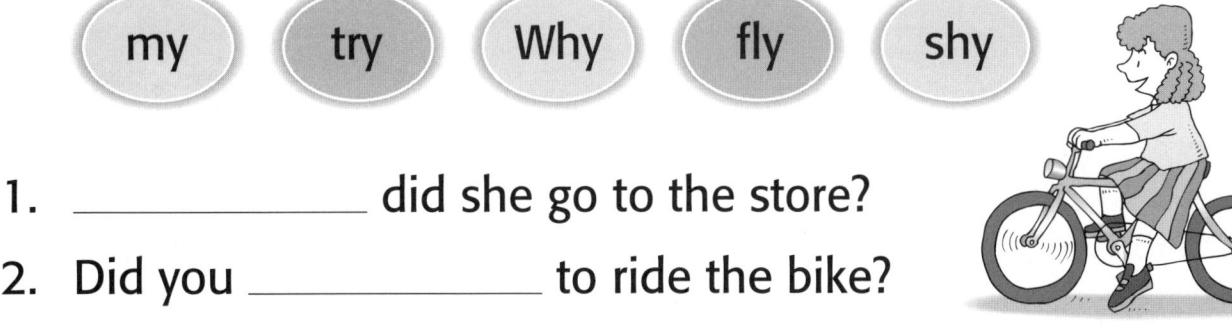

Past Tense Verbs

- Some verbs tell what happened in the past. You can add "ed" to them.

D. Read the crossword verbs. Add "ed" and write them in the correct places.

Across
A. plant
B. want
C. train
D. learn
E. ask

Down
1. treat
2. sail
3. play
4. answer
5. help
6. need

Months of the Year

E. Read the sentences below. Fill in the correct months.

October   July   January
June   November   April
December   February
March   May   August
September

1. In _____ , it is Christmas.

2. School starts in _____ .

3. Valentine's Day falls in _____ .

4. Halloween is at the end of _____ .

5. The first month of the year is _____ .

6. The month in which school ends for the summer vacation is _____ .

7. The eighth month of the year is _____ .

8. The second last month of the year is _____ .

9. The month in which St. Patrick's Day falls is _____ .

10. Easter usually occurs in _____ .

11. The name for this month rhymes with "day". _____

12. Canada Day is the first day of this month. _____

17 Penguins

A. Read the story. Write the correct answers in the blanks.

Penguins are birds that cannot fly but are good swimmers. They live in Antarctica and off the coasts of Africa and Australia. The smallest penguin is 40 cm tall. It is called the Blue Fairy. The tallest penguin is the Emperor, which is almost 120 cm tall.

Penguins feed on fish, squid, and small shrimp. They are the prey of leopard seals and killer whales. The female penguin lays an egg or two and goes off in search of food. While she is gone, the male hatches the eggs on his feet under a layer of fur.

1. Penguins live in _____ and off the coasts of _____ and _____ .

2. The smallest penguin is called the _____ .

3. It is _____ tall.

4. The tallest penguin is called the _____ , which is _____ tall.

5. Penguins feed on _____ , _____ , and _____ .

6. _____ and _____ prey on penguins.

7. The _____ lays the eggs and the _____ hatches them.

Phonics: Soft and Hard "g" and "c"

- The letters "g" and "c" have both hard and soft sounds.

    Examples: go (hard "g" sound); ginger (soft "g" sound)

    can (hard "c" sound); celery (soft "c" sound)

B. Read the words on the squares and place them in the correct blocks below.

 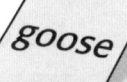   

1.

2.

3.

4.

Irregular Past Tense Verbs

- Some verbs don't end in "ed".
  Examples: sing ⟶ sang; speak ⟶ spoke

C. Match up the present and past tenses.

1.
drink	rang
write	saw
ring	went
say	wrote
see	drank
go	said

2.
give	ran
think	drove
ride	left
run	gave
drive	thought
leave	rode

3.
come	stood
swim	came
take	made
stand	swam
make	took
fly	flew

4.
lose	tried
have	spoke
hear	ate
try	lost
speak	had
eat	heard

Computers

We use computers everywhere – at school, at home, at the doctor's, the dentist's, and the department stores. It is important to know the main parts of the computer. The <u>monitor</u> is the screen that displays words and pictures. When you type on a <u>keyboard</u>, your words appear on the monitor. If you want a paper copy, you can use a <u>printer</u> to print the words or pictures. Some computers use <u>diskettes</u> to save work and others use <u>CDs</u>, which look the same as the ones you use to play music. If you add a <u>modem</u> to your computer, you can communicate with other people.

Word Search

D. Find the words that are underlined above.

i	m	m	o	n	i	t	o	r	c	d	e	b	f
a	f	o	u	n	d	i	s	k	e	t	t	e	s
h	n	j	p	r	i	n	t	e	r	a	l	b	o
u	d	k	d	b	i	a	b	y	o	f	e	u	a
k	a	o	e	a	u	e	u	b	h	c	j	i	k
a	p	r	u	f	b	r	m	o	d	e	m	b	d
q	h	i	c	t	d	s	c	a	o	n	e	r	l
c	d	r	o	m	s	t	j	r	d	k	e	l	h
j	i	j	v	s	i	w	o	d	h	g	s	k	t

PROGRESS TEST 2

A. Fill in the missing words from the word bank below.

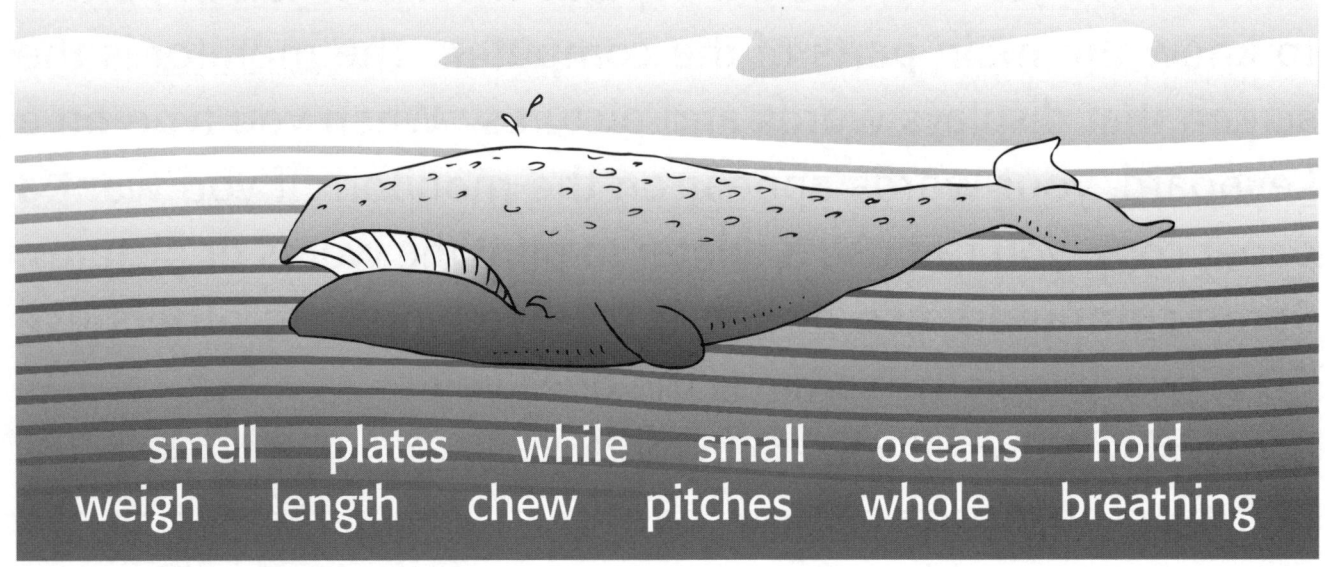

smell   plates   while   small   oceans   hold
weigh   length   chew   pitches   whole   breathing

Whales live in 1._____ throughout the world. Some whales have between 2 and 300 teeth, 2._____ others have no teeth at all. The whales that have no teeth feed on 3._____ organisms and use long bristles called 4._____ to eat them. Those that have teeth do not 5._____ their prey but eat them 6._____ .

Whales range in 7._____ from 1.3 metres to almost 30 metres. They 8._____ anywhere from 45 kg to 136,000 kg. Some whales have little sense of 9._____ and some none at all. Their hearing, however, allows them to hear 10._____ much higher than what we can hear.

Small whales can 11._____ their breath for several minutes, and larger ones stay underwater without 12._____ for many hours.

Proper and Common Nouns

A common noun names any person, place, or thing.
A proper noun names a specific person, place, or thing.

B. Read the story. Circle ◯ the common nouns. Underline the proper nouns.

David and his friend, Chris, are going to visit the Hockey Hall of Fame in downtown Toronto, Canada. It is in a large building not far from Union Station, where the friends are taking the subway from Mississauga to Toronto.

There are so many exciting exhibits at the Hockey Hall of Fame. There are pieces of equipment worn by famous hockey players, like Wayne Gretzky. The Stanley Cup, which is awarded to the top hockey team each year, is sometimes on display there.

The boys want to see the first mask that was worn by Jacques Plante and some of the old hockey uniforms from years gone by. Maybe, if they're lucky, they might see a visiting hockey player.

The last thing David and Chris go to see is all the statistics of players who broke many records over the years. Players like Gordie Howe, Jean Beliveau, and Wayne Gretzky changed the game of hockey forever.

Using Code

C. Use the code to fill in the blanks. Check the word bank to see if you are correct.

A	B	C	D	E	F	G	H	I	J	K	L	M	N	O	P	Q	R	S	T	U	V	W	X	Y	Z
1	2	3	4	5	6	7	8	9	10	11	12	13	14	15	16	17	18	19	20	21	22	23	24	25	26

Provinces and Territories

__ __ __ __ __ __ is one of the __ __ __ __ __ __ __ countries in
3 1 14 1 4 1   12 1 18 7 5 19 20

the __ __ __ __ __. It is one of __ __ __ __ countries that make
    23 15 18 12 4   20 8 18 5 5

up __ __ __ __ __ __ __ __ __ __ __. It is made up of __ __ __
   14 15 18 20 8   1 13 5 18 9 3 1   20 5 14

provinces and __ __ __ __ __ territories. __ __ __ __ __ __ __
              20 8 18 5 5   14 21 14 1 22 21 20

became the newest __ __ __ __ __ __ __ __ in 1999.
                   20 5 18 18 9 20 15 18 25

There are __ __ __ __ Atlantic provinces and __ __ __ __ __ of
           6 15 21 18   20 8 18 5 5

them are called __ __ __ __ __ __ __ __ provinces.
                13 1 18 9 20 9 13 5

There are also __ __ __ __ __ Prairie provinces.
                20 8 18 5 5

Word Bank

three　　world　　Nunavut　　three　　ten　　three
territory　　largest　　four　　North　　Canada　　Maritime
America　　three

Grammar Focus

D. Circle ◯ the correct answers.

1. Christina (go, went) to visit the Science Centre.
2. Maria (travels, is travelling) to the Philippines soon.
3. John (is, am) good at cooking.
4. Frank (like, likes) to watch football.
5. Rob (fix, fixes) his own car.
6. David (played, plays) his guitar every day.
7. Kathleen (studies, study) hard before her exams.
8. Patrick (skis, ski) with his friends.
9. Michael (will go, go) to the video store.
10. Elizabeth (tries, try) to take time to paint.
11. Christine (take, takes) the dog for a walk daily.
12. Will you (go, went) with your mom?
13. Did Kaitlin (bake, bakes) the cookies?
14. That clown (laugh, laughs) loudly.
15. They like to (watch, watches) television together.

Vocabulary Building

E. Circle ◯ the synonym for each word below.

Synonyms are words that have the same meaning.

1. big (small, **large**)
2. weep (sweep, **cry**)
3. small (**tiny**, big)
4. dash (**run**, walk)
5. unhappy (**sad**, cheery)
6. jump (**hop**, jog)

F. Underline the correct homonyms.

Homonyms are words that sound the same but have different meanings.

1. sail (sale, seal)
2. see (sea, say)
3. pair (pear, peal)
4. male (mail, mane)
5. blew (blue, blow)
6. vain (vane, van)

G. Draw squares around the correct antonyms.

Antonyms are words that have opposite meanings.

1. dark (night, **bright**)
2. wet (**dry**, wide)
3. dirty (**clean**, muddy)
4. open (**close**, wide)
5. sad (**happy**, mad)
6. light (**heavy**, easy)

Vowels that Sound Like "i" or "y"

H. Read the words in the boxes. Say them out loud. Circle ○ the "e" or "i" that it sounds like.

Section 2

Grammar

1 Nouns (1)

Parent Note:
Recognition of rhyming words is a precursor to reading. It is important to "play" with rhyming words orally.

Rhyming Nouns

A. Match the nouns that rhyme. Colour each pair the same colour.

swing	fox	ring	block
beet	lock	frog	hat
bat	bee	key	box
feet	log	fish	dish

Noun Word Families

B. Find the letters in the alphabet box that help you make new nouns.

a b c d e f g h i j k l m
n o p q r s t u v w x y z

1. _c_ at
   ___ at
   ___ at
   ___ at
   ___ at
   ___ at

2. _b_ ar
   ___ ar
   ___ ar
   ___ ___ ar

3. _f_ ig
   ___ ig
   ___ ig
   ___ ig

C. Spot the nouns. Circle ◯ the words that are nouns.

 cup

 candle

 balloon

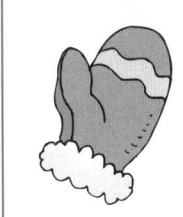 glove

 smile

 good

 lamp

hat

 flower

Categorizing Noun Groups

D. Look at each row of words. Colour the box with a noun that belongs to the same group as the one on the left.

1. apple	sink	pear	cat
2. boy	tree	dog	man
3. chair	lamp	cup	table
4. cat	box	dog	leaf
5. sun	flower	moon	rake
6. pan	pot	shoe	hat
7. shirt	orange	jacket	ball
8. gate	grass	plate	fence
9. pen	duck	pencil	balloon
10. star	sky	heart	lead
11. fish	ball	ocean	grape
12. key	door	needle	train
13. car	coat	truck	jar
14. hand	hat	band	finger

Identifying / Sorting Nouns

E. Look at the words in the box. Put them in the columns below.

```
boy          school        television
penguin      Ottawa        park
orange       man           glass
city         baby          Mr. Smith
girl         bike          Toronto
mother       sun           postman
balloon      Ontario       village
banana       candle        finger
Alberta      woman         Maria
lamp         radio         ring
doctor       Wonderland    town
```

Person	Place	Thing

2 Nouns (2)

Proper Nouns

A proper noun names a special person, place, or thing. Proper nouns always begin with a capital letter.

Examples: person – Mr. Jones
　　　　　　place – Canada
　　　　　　thing – CN Tower

A. Finish each sentence with a proper noun. Be sure to start the noun with a capital letter.

1. My favourite day of the week is _____ .

2. School begins in _____ . (month)

3. I live in _____ . (city or town)

4. My favourite teacher is _____ . (name)

5. My full name is _____ .

6. My favourite holiday is _____ .

7. The school I go to is _____ .

8. My best friend's name is _____ .

A proper noun names a special person, place, or thing. It begins with a capital letter. Countries, provinces, and cities all begin with capital letters.

B. Change the names of the provinces and cities that are meant to be capitalized. Write them in the word box.

- yukon
- toronto
- victoria
- regina
- st. john's
- halifax
- montreal
- canada
- edmonton
- winnipeg
- vancouver
- calgary
- quebec city
- fredericton
- ottawa

Common Nouns

A common noun names any person, place, or thing.
Examples: dog   book   boy   gift

C. Circle ◯ the common nouns in each sentence. Write the words in the word bank.

1. I saw a bright star in the sky.
2. The leaves on the tree are orange.
3. The cat has black fur.
4. There are seven days in a week.
5. The clock ticked away slowly.
6. Everyone got a good lunch.
7. She got the bus to the mall.
8. Did you get a new car?
9. The brown dog is on the rug.
10. How many photos did you take?

Word Bank

Proper and Common Noun Review

Remember: A common noun names any person, place, or thing. A proper noun names a special person, place, or thing.

D. Read the nouns. Write "P" for proper nouns. Write "C" for common nouns.

1. book   C
2. SkyDome   P
3. pen   ___
4. Mary   ___
5. cereal   ___
6. car   ___
7. tower   ___
8. Saturday   ___
9. dog   ___
10. CN Tower   ___
11. tree   ___
12. July   ___
13. goat   ___
14. Mr. Kirk   ___

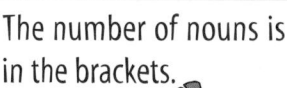

The number of nouns is in the brackets.

E. Underline the common nouns in these sentences. Circle ◯ the proper nouns.

1. School starts in September. (2)
2. Andrew likes to drive his car, Pepe. (3)
3. The CN Tower is the tallest building in Canada. (3)
4. I rode my bike down the path to Loblaws. (3)
5. Anne and Bob took their dog to the park. (4)
6. Tuesday is the third day of the week. (3)

3 Plural Nouns

 A plural noun names more than one person, place, or thing. You can make most nouns plural by adding "s".

Example: She read one book.
She read ten book**s**.

A. Write the singular nouns (one) and plural nouns (more than one) in the correct boxes.

cat   cup   pan   bees   finger   dogs
gate   chair   can   cake   bag
apples   pots   bug   faces   grape
trees   tables   bottle   cookies

One (singular)	More than one (plural)

Distinguishing between "s" and "es"

You can make a noun plural by adding "es" if the noun ends in "x" or "s" or just add "s" to most nouns.

B. Help Maria get to the shoes by filling in "s" or "es".

| box _es_ | tree _s_ | ax _es_ |
| kiss _es_ |
| cake _s_ | book _s_ | yard _s_ | hand _s_ |
| bike _s_ |
| flower _s_ | bag _s_ | pass _es_ | tax _es_ |
| bus _es_ |
| fox _es_ | glass _es_ | mix _es_ | car _s_ |
| gas _es_ |
| park _s_ | cookie _s_ | dream _s_ | mitten _s_ |
| egg _s_ |
| shop _s_ | coat _s_ | bed _s_ |

Nouns Ending in "ch" or "sh"

Nouns that end in "ch" or "sh" are made plural by adding "es".
Examples: church → church**es**
fi**sh** → fish**es**

C. Read the words below. Print them in the correct column and fill in the missing nouns.

wishes   brush   patch   lunches   bench

One	More than one
dish 	dishes 

D. Make the nouns plural.

1. I like _____ . (peach)

2. My mom gives me _____ every day. (kiss)

3. She made two _____ on her birthday. (wish)

4. The _____ are on the road. (church)

5. There were several _____ in the tank. (fish)

Noun Riddles

E. Read the clues below. Choose the noun that fits each clue best and write the answer in the blank.

book   bike   car   chair
orange   bus   sun   fingers
refrigerator   snow
McDonald's   eyes

1. I am something to sit on. _____
2. I am good to read. _____
3. Your mom and dad drive me. _____
4. Some children go to school in me. _____
5. Lots of kids like to eat here. _____
6. I keep food cold in the kitchen. _____
7. You can ride me. _____
8. There are five of me on each hand. _____
9. I am cold and fall from the sky in winter. _____
10. I am orange, juicy, and good to eat. _____
11. You can see with me. _____
12. I keep the Earth warm and bright. _____

4 Pronouns

Pronouns (I, me, we, us)

A pronoun is a word that is used in place of a noun.
"I" is a pronoun that is always capitalized.

A. Read each sentence. Fill in the blank with the correct pronoun.

1. _____ go to school every day. (I, me)
2. My mom took _____ to the movies. (I, me)
3. _____ all went to the playground. (we, us)
4. The driver took _____ to the market. (we, us)
5. Will you give _____ the ticket? (I, me)
6. _____ am riding my bike. (I, me)
7. Mary bought _____ a ball. (I, me)
8. _____ are going to take a holiday. (we, us)
9. The teacher taught _____ to read. (we, us)

B. Write a sentence using the pronoun.

1. I _____
2. we _____
3. us _____

Pronouns (you, he, him, she, her)

"He" and "him" are pronouns that refer to boys and men.
"She" and "her" are pronouns that refer to girls and women.
"You" is a pronoun that refers to the person(s) one is talking or writing to.

C. Choose one of the two pronouns to fill in each blank.

The Pumpkin Farm

Julie went on a school trip to the pumpkin farm. 1. _____ (She, He) got on the bus at school with 2. _____ (her, him) friends. 3. _____ (She, He) had lots of fun singing songs and talking to 4. _____ (she, her) friends.

When 5. _____ (she, he) arrived at the farm, the farmer told 6. _____ (her, him) all about how pumpkins grew from a tiny seed. 7. _____ (She, He) gave 8. _____ (her, him) some toasted pumpkin seeds to eat. Then, 9. _____ (she, he) took the children out to the pumpkin patch.

10. _____ (She, He) helped Julie choose a pumpkin of 11. _____ (her, she) own to take home.

Pronouns (it, they, them)

The pronoun "it" can refer to one place or thing.
The pronouns "they" and "them" refer to more than one person, place, or thing.

D. Read the words or phrases in Column A. Draw a line to connect them with the correct pronouns in Column B.

Column A

1. Mary and Jim
2. the spider
3. all the dogs
4. a balloon
5. the moon
6. Julie and her mom
7. Andrew went with ___ .
8. ___ have two cars.
9. James got ___ fixed.
10. Tina and Sherry
11. my friends

Column B

they
they
them
they
they
it
it
it
them
They
they

Pronoun Review

E. Choose the correct pronoun from the word bank and write it in the blank. Put a line through the pronoun when you use it.

> They   It   She   It   they   them
> her   his   You   it   them   he

1. The boys like apples. _____ eat _____ every day.

2. Karen can skate well. _____ practises weekly.

3. My dog has a leash. _____ wears _____ on our walks.

4. My TV is broken. _____ needs to be fixed.

5. The pages got wet when _____ fell into the water.

6. Cindy is taking _____ bike to school.

7. James put on _____ helmet.

8. Libby likes movies; she watches _____ a lot.

9. "_____ should listen carefully," the teacher said.

10. When _____ took off the hat, John's hair was messy.

5 Verbs (1)

A verb is an action word that tells what a person, place, or thing does. It is often a physical action – one that you can see.

A. Choose a verb from the word bank that matches each picture. Write the verb in the blank.

throws   walk   draw   runs   play
skates   drinks   bakes   sings

Example: Joe ___rides___ his bike.

1. Judy _____ to the park.

2. They _____ to school every day.

3. Jim _____ lots of water every day.

4. Mom _____ cookies on the weekend.

5. I _____ during art class.

6. Lori _____ marathons.

7. John _____ in the shower.

8. The boys _____ basketball in the driveway.

9. Ian _____ the ball to Mark.

Some verbs tell about actions you cannot see.
Example: Jim **thinks** he **knows** the answer.

B. Read the verbs in the word bank. Write them in the correct space.

go   eat   run   start   see   get   talk
try   sleep   learn   make   drive
cook   look   play   listen   work   touch
walk   hear   think   ask   do   write
watch   feel   throw   move

Can See 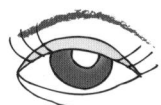	**Cannot See** 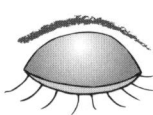

Naming Verbs

C. Look at each picture. Write the verb that matches.

> blowing   swinging   climbing
> falling   skating   growing

1. _____

2. _____

3. _____

4. _____

5. _____

6. _____

D. Underline the verb in each sentence.

1. The lamp shines all night.
2. Candles burn brightly.
3. Jimmy likes the cake.
4. I eat good food.
5. The mother rocks her baby.

Recognizing / Identifying Verbs

E. Read each sentence. Underline the verb. Write "S" if you can see the action and "C" if you cannot.

A verb tells about an action you can see (like drinking) or cannot see (like thinking).

1. Betty walks on the sidewalk. _____
2. Kurt talked to his friend. _____
3. James listens to the radio. _____
4. Mommy feels ill today. _____
5. Colin learns to play the piano. _____
6. Frances cooks dinner. _____
7. Vince drives his car to work. _____
8. Ben looked at the stars. _____
9. Do you see the clouds? _____
10. I think I can do that! _____

6 Verbs (2)

Regular Past Tense Verbs

A regular past tense verb tells what happened in the past and has "ed" added to it.

Examples: We **walk** to school. (present)
We **walked** to school. (past)

Past Tense Crossword

A. Read the present tense verb clues. Write them in the correct spaces, adding "ed" to each one.

Across

1. paint
2. pull
3. wish
4. kick
5. play
6. sew

Down

A. talk
B. walk
C. crawl

Irregular Past Tense Verbs

 Some verbs do not end in "ed".
Examples: sleep → slept   drink → drank

B. Match the present and past tense verbs.

say	•	• drove	drink	•	• made
ring	•	• swam	stand	•	• took
drive	•	• said	run	•	• drank
lose	•	• rang	take	•	• ran
swim	•	• lost	make	•	• stood

C. Read each sentence. Change the present tense verb to past tense.

flew   left   had   saw   stood   wrote

1. They have a nice house. _____
2. Bill and Cathy see the building. _____
3. They leave at noon. _____
4. They write to each other. _____
5. Jim and John stand by each other. _____
6. They fly on Air Canada. _____

Linking Verbs - Present Tense (is, am, are)

> Linking verbs tell what someone or something is.
> "Am" is used when you talk about yourself. (I **am**)
> "Is" is used when you are talking about one. (singular)
> "Are" is used when you are talking about more than one. (plural)

D. Read each sentence. Fill in the blank with "am", "is", or "are".

1. The weather _____ fine today.
2. I _____ a good student.
3. Her grandmother _____ a seamstress.
4. Clare and Nicole _____ good friends.
5. I _____ sure they will drive us.
6. Jeffrey _____ good at running.
7. Sheri and Dean _____ nice people.
8. They _____ afraid to walk outside after dark.
9. Her mother _____ angry with her.
10. Their dad _____ happy to see them.
11. Sandra and I _____ sisters.

Some sentences use "is" and "are" to tell about what someone **is** or what some people **are** doing.

Examples: Sean **is** playing baseball. (singular – one)
Mary and Steve **are** playing golf.
(plural – more than one)

E. Read each sentence. Fill in the blanks with "is" or "are".

1. Sanjeep _____ working at the store.
2. Julia and Angelie _____ going to the movie.
3. Daniel and Anne Marie _____ hiking to the river.
4. Herman _____ taking the bus to work.
5. Frances and her daughters _____ going shopping.
6. We _____ trying to learn a new language.
7. Tony _____ swimming in the pool.
8. They _____ waiting to board the train.
9. Tom and Lorraine _____ visiting their friends.
10. Maria _____ drawing her favourite pet.
11. The children _____ watching a cartoon.
12. The boys _____ playing an exciting game of hockey.

7 Verbs (3)

Linking Verbs - Past Tense (was, were)

When an action has already happened, the linking verbs "is", "am", and "are" become "was" and "were".

Examples:

Present	Past
I am working.	I **was** working.
You are working.	You **were** working.
He is working.	He **was** working.

A. Read each sentence. Choose the correct word in parentheses ( ) and write it in the blank.

1. The weather _____ fine yesterday. (is, was)
2. The van _____ washed last week. (is, was)
3. Sheri and Jean _____ walking to town when it rained. (are, were)
4. Tricia _____ given a new book. (was, were)

B. Write the past tense of these linking verbs.

Present
1. is helping
2. are cooking
3. am sewing
4. is walking
5. are baking

Past
_____ helping
_____ cooking
_____ sewing
_____ walking
_____ baking

Helping Verbs

Many verbs are made up of 2 or 3 words.

Usually, the last word is the main verb. The other words are helping verbs.

The most common helping verbs are forms of "be", "have", and "do".

Examples:

Helping Verb	Main Verb	Verb
am	cooking	am cooking
have	cooked	have cooked
did	cook	did cook

C. Read each sentence. Write the helping verb and the main verb in the spaces.

Sentence	Helping Verb	Main Verb
Example: Jimmy is helping his mom.	is	helping
1. Susan has talked to her son.		
2. Maria has visited the Philippines.		
3. Daniel and Anne Marie are hiking to the woods.		
4. Jane did give Sean the book yesterday.		
5. Ben is walking his dogs.		
6. John had worked on the bike.		

Linking and Helping Verbs

D. This story contains linking and helping verbs in the present tense. Read the story. Choose the correct words and fill in the blanks.

A Visit to the Farm

Su Lin and Mai 1._____ (is, are) going to visit a farm with their grandparents. They 2._____ (is, are) packing the things they need to take with them. Mai 3._____ (have, has) taken out the blue suitcase and 4._____ (have, has) placed it on the bed. She 5._____ (is, are) looking for the clothes she'll need. She 6._____ (is, are) hoping to be able to 7._____ (feed, feeds) the pigs, so she 8._____ (is, are) getting out her old pants and boots.

Su Lin 9._____ (is, are) hoping to go horseback riding at the farm. She 10._____ (is, are) planning to get a helmet tomorrow. She 11._____ (is, are) also packing a swimsuit because she 12._____ (like, likes) to swim.

Verb Review

Verbs are words that tell of an action you can see or, sometimes, not see. Some verbs are links, like "is", "am", and "are". Some verbs use "is" and "are" to help them.

E. Read the sentences. Fill in the blanks.

> bought   wind   took   opened
> was   were   wound   is flying   is
> flew   packed   left   brought

1. Spring _____ a good season for kite flying.
2. We _____ a new kite.
3. We _____ our kite to the park to fly it.
4. The kite _____ up high above the trees.
5. We had to _____ the string around a roller.
6. When the kite _____ very high, we _____ out of string.
7. Janie yelled, "Look, how high it _____ ."
8. We _____ our mouths with surprise.
9. Later, we _____ our kite down.
10. We _____ the string around the roller.
11. We _____ up and _____ the park.

Progress Test 1

Noun Match-up

A. Help Tony Turtle find his way to the pond by writing under the pictures the nouns that match.

Nouns

Remember: A noun names a person, place, or thing.

B. Match the noun to the picture. Draw a line to connect them.

1. 2. 3. 4. 5. 6.

cup   ring   log   milk   pan   sun

Word Families

C. Write the letters that help you create new nouns.

1. cat	2. dog	3. jug
___ at	___ og	___ ug
___ at	___ og	___ ug
___ at	___ og	___ ug
___ at	___ og	___ ug

Progress Test 1

Proper and Common Nouns

A proper noun names a specific person, place, or thing (and begins with a capital letter). A common noun names any person, place, or thing.

D. Circle ◯ the proper nouns and underline the common nouns in these sentences.

1. Marie and James rode their bikes to the park.
2. Mr. Long is going to see the baseball game at the SkyDome on Tuesday.
3. The magician waved his wand at the audience and then disappeared behind a cloud of smoke.
4. Rudy, the hedgehog, lived in the garage under the wooden chips.
5. Andrew took the bus to Main Street.
6. The boat sailed on Lake Ontario.
7. My favourite movie is *Peter Pan*.
8. There were many dogs at the Credit Valley Pet Hospital.
9. Did your mom go to Toronto?
10. It was a nice day at Wonderland.

Pronouns

Remember: A pronoun is a word that can take the place of a noun. I, me, we, us, you, he, him, she, her, it, they, and them are pronouns.

E. Change the sentences by replacing the underlined nouns with pronouns.

1. <u>Derek</u> has a new car.

   _____ has a new car. (She, He)

2. <u>Marie</u> bought a chocolate bar.

   _____ bought a chocolate bar. (She, He)

3. <u>The cat</u> climbed the tree.

   _____ climbed the tree. (It, They)

4. <u>Jose</u> and <u>Carlos</u> like to play ball.

   _____ like to play ball. (It, They)

5. <u>John</u> wants to play hockey this season.

   _____ wants to play hockey this season.

   (She, He)

6. Please hang <u>your coat</u> on the hook.

   Please hang _____ on the hook. (them, it)

Verbs

Remember: Some verbs are words about an action, like "running", "walking", "playing", and "flying". Some verbs are words about thinking, feeling, tasting, smelling, and other actions you cannot see.

F. In the word search below, find the verbs from the word list.

fly   climb   think   run   ride   smell
talk   play   jump   slide   swim   drink

a	p	a	r	w	u	a	s	h	v	f	t	r	h	e
n	r	c	e	a	r	r	i	d	e	l	h	s	j	i
c	l	i	m	b	a	t	u	s	n	y	s	f	e	k
l	e	l	i	l	d	m	c	o	c	w	v	c	t	l
o	u	d	s	q	l	s	v	b	h	b	x	s	d	t
k	s	h	w	r	r	u	n	r	s	h	t	a	l	k
s	v	v	i	o	f	g	k	i	c	k	h	m	a	f
u	f	s	m	t	g	u	s	v	u	t	i	h	e	f
v	s	r	f	s	d	r	i	n	k	e	n	s	p	s
h	m	a	l	k	n	t	s	p	s	v	k	c	j	y
u	e	t	h	a	o	b	e	l	k	o	m	e	u	a
r	l	h	i	k	t	c	p	l	a	y	b	f	m	d
s	l	i	d	e	s	d	l	h	t	r	l	t	p	s

> Verbs are words that tell what is happening — an action that is mental or physical. The past tense of regular verbs have "ed" added.

G. Underline the correct word in the parentheses ( ) in each sentence.

1. She (move, moved) to another house in the town.
2. Frances (touch, touched) the surface to see if it was wet.
3. Did you (watch, watched) TV last night?
4. Jim (work, worked) on his car all day.
5. I (watch, watched) my favourite TV show every day.

H. Underline the verbs (action words).

1. Marcie learned a new language.
2. Did you try to climb the tree?
3. My mom cooks good meals for us.
4. I can make a house of cards.
5. Leslie talks on the phone all the time.
6. Tracy makes her own clothes.

8 Adjectives

An adjective is a word that tells something about a noun (person, place, or thing).

Example: Jane patted the **shaking** dog.

A. Choose an adjective from the word bank to match the picture.

bright   rainy   thin   high   hard   dirty

   1. a _____ man

2. the _____ sun

   3. the _____ clothes

4. a _____ day

   5. a _____ mountain

6. the _____ wood

B. Complete each sentence below with the adjective that fits.

1. The _____ man lifted the barbells.
2. The _____ glass shone.
3. The _____ bike lay on the grass.
4. The _____ candle burned slowly.

shiny
strong
broken
orange

Adjectives - Size and Shape

Words that describe or tell more about people, places, or things (nouns) are called adjectives. Some adjectives describe size and shape.

Examples: a **big** dog   a **small** toy   a **tiny** rock   a **round** ball

C. The adjectives below describe size or shape. Circle ◯ the adjectives that describe size and underline the adjectives that describe shape.

1. short
2. square
3. tiny
4. wide
5. tall
6. large
7. oval
8. huge
9. round
10. sharp
11. long
12. high

D. Fill in the blanks with suitable adjectives from above.

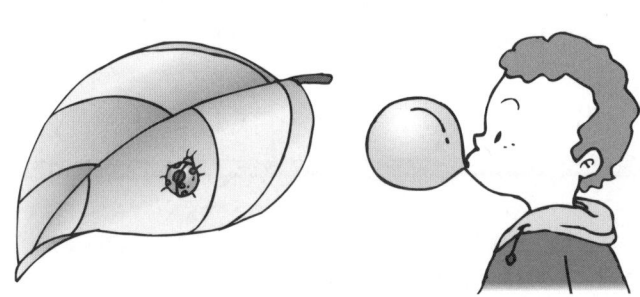

1. a _____ table
2. a _____ knife
3. a _____ bug
4. a _____ bubble
5. a _____ pencil
6. a _____ building

Adjectives - Colour and Number

Some adjectives describe the colour of something or the number.

Examples: the **blue** balloon   the **red** car
several balloons   **ten** cars

E. Find six words that describe colour in the word search.

e	n	h	m	h	b	l	c	k	s	r	a	r	y
m	f	q	e	g	c	k	b	o	r	a	n	g	e
t	r	j	a	r	e	d	h	l	u	h	v	h	l
b	b	l	u	e	r	m	u	r	l	m	d	l	l
d	q	r	t	e	h	b	l	a	c	k	e	k	o
e	s	t	v	n	j	d	s	r	t	t	a	i	w

F. Fill in the blanks with adjectives for colour or number.

1. My mom gave me a new _____ coat. (colour)

2. The tree is a pretty _____ colour in the fall. (colour)

3. They gave _____ dollars to the needy. (number)

4. I often eat _____ apples a day. (number)

5. My sister is _____ years old today. (number)

Adjective Review

Adjectives are words that describe or tell about nouns.
Some adjectives describe how something looks, sounds, tastes, feels, or smells.

G. Circle ◯ the adjective in each of these phrases.

1. a (dusty) drawer
2. a (delicious) aroma
3. (green) beans
4. a (rough) fabric
5. (juicy) fruit
6. a (sharp) knife
7. (sweet) gum
8. (salty) French fries
9. a (loud) sound
10. (brown) gravy

H. Think of adjectives that you know and write them in the correct boxes.

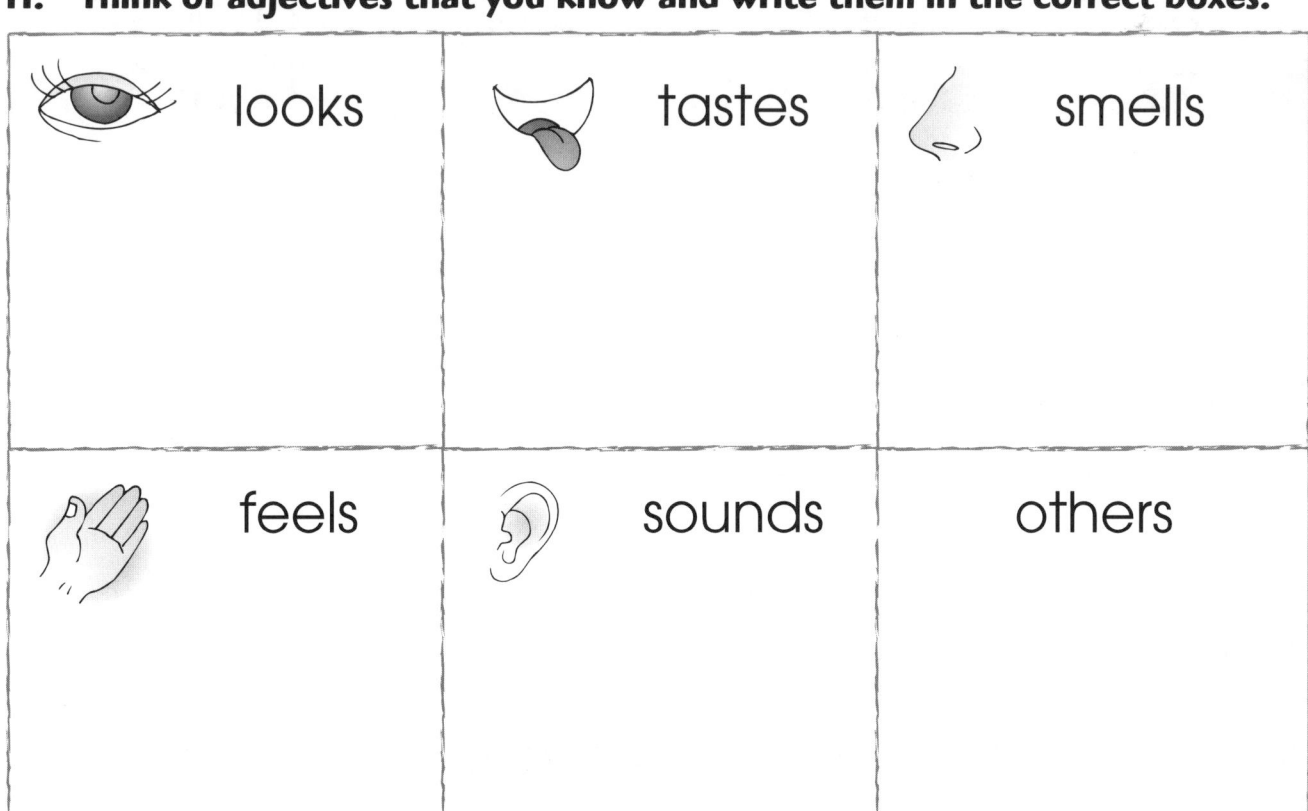

9 Articles

Articles (a, an)

An article is a "helping" word. It comes before a noun.
"A" is a word that is used before a noun that begins with a consonant.
"An" is a word that is used before a noun that begins with a vowel.

Examples: **a** house   **a** bear   **a** doll
             an egg   **an** animal   **an** ox

A. Choose the correct article for each noun. Fill in "a" or "an".

1. ____ radio
2. ____ oven
3. ____ shoe
4. ____ candle
5. ____ otter
6. ____ chair
7. ____ aunt
8. ____ boat
9. ____ bag
10. ____ table
11. ____ apple
12. ____ octopus

B. Fill in "a" or "an" to complete the sentences.

1. The otter is ____ animal that lives in water.
2. Laura and Jim are building ____ sand castle.
3. It is ____ sunny day in July.
4. My dog chewed ____ old shoe.
5. The tree grew in the woods near ____ village.

Articles (the)

"The" is used before a noun that names a particular person, place, or thing.

Examples: **The** king issued a decree.
They went to **the** zoo.

C. Choose "a", "an", or "the" to fill in the blanks.

a   an   the

1. _____ children visited _____ park.
2. I want to fly _____ airplane.
3. She had _____ itch on her knee.
4. _____ farm had lots of pigs.
5. _____ ant crawled up my arm.
6. My family went on _____ trip on _____ airplane.
7. Jenny took _____ dog to _____ vet.
8. Colin walked to _____ playground with his friend.
9. Mike is riding _____ bike to school.
10. Mom cleaned out _____ attic in our house.

Parts of Speech Review

D. Write any word you like for the following parts of speech.

1. proper noun – person	
2. adjective – colour	
3. verb – present tense	
4. adjective – size	
5. verb – past tense	
6. common noun – place	
7. verb – helping	
8. article – an	

E. Use the words you wrote above to write sentences.

1. _____
2. _____
3. _____
4. _____
5. _____
6. _____
7. _____
8. _____

F. Read each sentence. Look at the underlined word. Fill in "N" if the word is a noun. Fill in "P" if the word is a pronoun. Fill in "V" if the word is a verb. Fill in "A" if the word is an adjective.

1. Juan has a <u>black</u> cat. _____
2. Mario went to the <u>store</u>. _____
3. I am riding <u>my</u> bike. _____
4. Pierre <u>skates</u> very well. _____
5. Did you go to the <u>concert</u>? _____
6. The bus <u>stopped</u> at all the stops. _____
7. The girl <u>wished</u> she were a star. _____
8. <u>He</u> kicked the can down the street. _____
9. When are you getting your <u>new</u> shoes? _____
10. It is not <u>her</u> turn. _____

G. Fill in the blanks. Choose the articles that fit.

1. The boy took _____ apple from the table. (a, an)
2. We reached _____ store on time. (a, the)
3. Do you have more of _____ books? (a, the)
4. It was _____ actor in a costume. (a, an)
5. I want to go to _____ beach. (an, the)
6. If you go, take _____ dog with you. (a, the)
7. I see _____ new star in the sky. (a, an)

10 Recognizing Sentences

A sentence is a group of words that tells a complete idea.
Examples: (Sentence) June is the sixth month of the year.
(Non-sentence) June is month

A. Read the following groups of words aloud. Write "S" for a sentence and "N" for a non-sentence.

1. The fly
2. A chair has four legs and a back.
3. Toronto is the capital of Ontario.
4. Storms coming
5. The rain fell on the cars and houses.
6. A baby cat is called a kitten.
7. My baby sister Jane
8. Leaves turn colour in the fall.
9. The circus is
10. Many boys and girls like to swing.
11. We draw pictures.
12. The blue sky

B. **Match the beginning of each sentence with the ending. Write the letters.**

1. Most trees ☐
2. Baseball bats ☐
3. Popsicles ☐
4. Ice ☐
5. Baby horses ☐
6. My pencil ☐
7. Birds fly ☐
8. Boxes are good ☐
9. It often snows ☐
10. The children ☐
11. The baby ☐
12. We often swim ☐

A. is chubby.
B. are six years old.
C. are called foals.
D. for carrying things.
E. in winter.
F. have green leaves.
G. in summer.
H. is on the floor.
I. in the sky.
J. are made of wood.
K. is cold.
L. are cold and sweet.

Word Order

When you change the word order of a sentence, you can change the meaning.

Examples: The cat is on the hat.   The hat is on the cat.

C. Look at each picture and underline the sentence that gives the correct meaning.

1. The river is over the bridge.
   The bridge is over the river.

2. The ball is on the grass.
   The grass is on the ball.

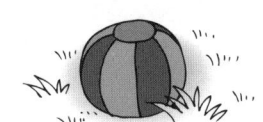

3. The boat is on the water.
   The water is on the boat.

4. The butterfly is on the flower.
   The flower is on the butterfly.

5. The rabbit chases the fox.
   The fox chases the rabbit.

6. The egg is on the plate.
   The plate is on the egg.

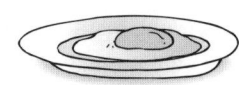

7. The apple is in front of the pear.
   The pear is in front of the apple.

8. The glass is in the water.
   The water is in the glass.

D. Put the words in order to make meaningful sentences.

1. big is lion The .
   _____

2. have I a bike .
   _____

3. play The boys baseball .
   _____

4. Pat a rabbit has cute .
   _____

5. Sam likes shoes blue the .
   _____

6. have a swing We in our backyard .
   _____

11 Sentence Types

Statements

A statement is a sentence that tells something. It begins with a capital and ends with a period.

A. Write "S" if the sentence is a statement. Write "NS" if the sentence is not a statement.

1. Did you go to summer camp? _____
2. We went to a riding camp. _____
3. The lakes there are beautiful. _____
4. Did you row the boat? _____
5. We took the short cut. _____

B. Draw a line to match the words in A with the words in B to make statements.

A
1. Rabbits
2. Bears
3. A pig
4. Monkeys
5. Cats
6. Horses

B
- live in barns.
- live in houses.
- live in burrows.
- live in dens.
- live in jungles.
- lives in a sty.

Questions

A question is a sentence that asks something.
A question begins with a capital and ends with a question mark (?).

C. Write "Q" if the sentence is a question. Write "NQ" if the sentence is not a question.

1. Do you like to swim? _____
2. She swims every day. _____
3. Her mother likes to shop. _____
4. Do you like to shop? _____
5. How many sisters do you have? _____

D. Finish the questions by writing the letters on the lines.

> A. on television?
> B. a new dress?
> C. the guitar?
> D. there in Canada?
> E. of Canada?
> F. travel on her vacation?

1. Have you ever played _____
2. How many provinces are _____
3. What is the capital _____
4. Where did she _____
5. Did you see the show _____
6. Will you buy _____

Exclamations

An exclamation is a sentence that shows strong feeling. It starts with a capital and ends with an exclamation mark (!).
Examples: Help! That's great!

E. Write "E" if the sentence is an exclamation. Write "NE" if the sentence is not an exclamation.

1. Wow, what a sunset! _____
2. Did you see that train? _____
3. I'm amazed! _____
4. It's not a mouse. _____
5. That sounds great! _____

F. Read the sentence. Add an exclamation mark (!), a question mark (?), or a period (.) if you think it fits.

1. Ouch
2. Help me, please
3. I never go there
4. Just try it
5. Wow
6. I'm so scared
7. I wish I could
8. Do you know her
9. Did you try it
10. You surprised me
11. Oh, no
12. Did you go
13. How wonderful
14. I want some water

Commands

 A command is a sentence that tells someone to do something.

G. Write "C" if the sentence is a command. Write "NC" if the sentence is not a command.

1. Don't take that chair. _____
2. Pick up your clothes, please. _____
3. You don't know if you don't try. _____
4. Take out the garbage, please. _____
5. Did you take the cookie? _____

H. Draw a line from A to the words in B that make the sentence a command.

A	B
1. Be	to eat your dinner.
2. Take	your doll here.
3. Try	a good girl.
4. Be	have some cake.
5. Bring	right there!
6. Girls,	very careful!
7. Stop	me to your leader!

12 Sentences

Subjects

The subject of a sentence tells **who** or **what** a sentence is about.
Example: **A tree** is a living thing.

A. Circle ◯ the subjects.

1. The tree has roots, a trunk, limbs, and leaves.
2. Most plants need light and water to grow.
3. The sun is the main source of light.
4. Rain gives plants the water they need.

B. Fill in the blanks with subjects from the word bank.

Roots   The stem   The fruit
Leaves   Plants

1. _____ have four main parts.
2. _____ take food and nutrients from the soil.
3. _____ is like a straw that helps the nutrients travel.
4. _____ make food for the plant.
5. _____ is where the seeds for new plants are stored.

Predicates

The predicate is the part of a sentence that tells something about the subject.

Example: Mark **likes to ride horses.**

C. Write the predicates of the sentences on the lines.

1. Mark brushes his horse's hair.
   _____

2. Horses like to be patted.
   _____

3. Most horses need to be trained.
   _____

4. Trainers talk to the horses.
   _____

D. Finish each of the sentences with a predicate.

1. Many children _____
2. My dad _____
3. My mom _____
4. I _____
5. My dog _____
6. My teacher _____

Subjects and Predicates

E. **Look at the picture and write predicates for the sentences.**

1. The children _____
   _____

2. The boy _____
   _____

3. The girl _____

4. I (Tim) _____

F. **Circle ◯ the subject and underline the predicate of each sentence.**

1. Clare and James like to play video games.

2. Marie went to the movie.

3. Tom bought an ice cream cone.

4. Colin waited for the bus.

5. Jorge likes to cook.

6. Melissa will take her friends with her.

7. The sun came out from behind the clouds.

8. We go for a walk every day.

9. Bears sleep in the winter.

10. Monopoly is my favourite game.

G. **Look at the picture. Write a subject to match what is happening. Make up your own names for the children.**

1. _____ are visiting the zoo.
2. _____ is looking at the tiger.
3. _____ is talking to the panda.
4. _____ is acting like a monkey.

H. **Underline the predicate in each sentence.**

1. The tiger is looking at the boy.
2. The zookeeper is feeding the elephant.
3. The panda is big.
4. The animals are lovely.
5. The children are very happy.

13 Punctuation and Capitalization

The first word in a sentence begins with a capital.
The important words in a title begin with capitals.

Examples: **T**he tree has a large trunk.
My favourite book is **V**elveteen **R**abbit.

A. Change the letters to capitals where they fit.

1. we read goldilocks and the three bears at school.

   _____

2. there are many boats on the sea.

   _____

3. i read the berenstein bears at school today.

   _____

4. do you like peter pan?

   _____

B. Write the titles of 2 of your favourite books.

_____

_____

C. Write the titles of 2 of your favourite movies.

D. Read the mixed up words. Put them in order.

Remember that a sentence begins with a capital letter.

1. apples are the turning red
   _____.
2. milkshake chocolate tastes the good
   _____.
3. a goat baby is kid a
   _____.
4. you do what know rabbit baby is a
   _____?
5. ate at we lunch restaurant the
   _____.
6. movie wow , great what a
   _____!
7. hope come you I too
   _____.
8. you want pie some do
   _____?
9. can't I wait
   _____!

Sentence Endings

A statement ends with a period (.).
A question ends with a question mark (?).
An exclamation ends with an exclamation mark (!).

Examples: The boy is tall .
Is the boy tall ?
Boy, is **he** tall !

E. Add the correct punctuation marks.

1. Wow, I am so excited ☐
2. Did you go to the show ☐
3. Do you like to eat pizza ☐
4. I wish I had a dog ☐
5. Oh no ☐
6. Where did they take you ☐
7. I had a little dream ☐
8. What's that ☐
9. I can't believe it ☐
10. Will you come back soon ☐
11. My baby brother is cute ☐
12. I love the story ☐

Sentence Beginnings and Endings

All sentences begin with capital letters. Some sentences end with a period " . ". Questions end with a " ? " and exclamations end with an " ! ".

F. Use the jumbled words to make sentences that have periods, exclamation marks, or question marks.

1. _____

2. _____

3. _____

4. _____

14 Sentence Type Review

A. Read each sentence. Decide if it is a statement (S) or an exclamation (E). Write "S" or "E" on the line and fill in the box with the correct punctuation.

1. _____ The bus was late ☐
2. _____ Thanks a lot ☐
3. _____ Ouch, I hurt my finger ☐
4. _____ The chair is too small ☐
5. _____ Oh no ☐

B. Read each sentence. Decide if it is a question (Q) or a command (C). Write "Q" or "C" on the line and fill in the box with the correct punctuation.

1. _____ Give me that box ☐
2. _____ Do you like it here ☐
3. _____ Will you please take me ☐
4. _____ Don't go there ☐
5. _____ What if I like it ☐
6. _____ Have you seen her ☐
7. _____ Take me to your teacher ☐

Subjects and Predicates

Examples: Subject – **Canada** has 10 provinces.
Predicate – Canada **has two official languages**.

C. Write the subject on the line below each sentence.

1. Janet wrote a funny song.
   _____

2. The song is called *The Happy Puppy*.
   _____

3. We sing the song with Mrs. Johnson.
   _____

4. Mrs. Johnson is our new music teacher.
   _____

5. She likes *The Happy Puppy* very much.
   _____

D. Write a predicate for each subject.

1. Little Tom _____
2. Bananas _____
3. Dad _____
4. The fish _____
5. The children _____

Sentence Beginnings and Endings

E. Read the scrambled sentences. Rewrite each sentence, using the correct beginning and proper punctuation.

1. Mary Joan bikes their and ride
   _____

2. Tracy many good friends has
   _____

3. are there girls class lots of her in
   _____

4. like chew dogs to bones
   _____

5. cousins my coming are visit a for
   _____

6. go vacation summer on we the in
   _____

7. wish cook I could I
   _____

8. books new bought she
   _____

9. gave cookie mom her a
   _____

10. bit apple I into the
    _____

Proofreading

F. Each of the following sentences has mistakes. Find the mistakes and write the sentence correctly.

1. Jordan and jim went camping (2 mistakes)

2. the girls tried to find the cat (2 mistakes)

3. every dollar counts (2 mistakes)

4. rainbows are a sign of good luck (2 mistakes)

5. did you like the candy (2 mistakes)

6. how are you today (2 mistakes)

7. give me the ruler (2 mistakes)

8. don't go there (2 mistakes)

9. take it with you (2 mistakes)

10. where are you going (2 mistakes)

Progress Test 2

Recognizing / Identifying Nouns

A. Write "N" in front of the words that are nouns.

1. ___ train
2. ___ school
3. ___ Toronto
4. ___ baby
5. ___ book
6. ___ chair
7. ___ town
8. ___ sing
9. ___ take
10. ___ give
11. ___ heart
12. ___ pencil
13. ___ cookie
14. ___ scarf
15. ___ short
16. ___ Jeff
17. ___ hot
18. ___ blue

B. Write the word that names the noun in each picture.

1.  _____
2. _____
3. _____
4. _____

5.  _____
6.  _____
7.  _____
8.  _____

9.  _____
10. 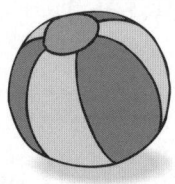 _____
11. 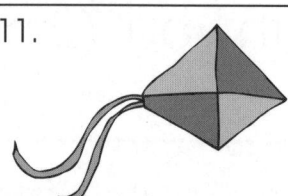 _____
12.  _____

Pronouns (I, me, we, us, you, he, him, she, her)

C. Complete the sentences with pronouns.

1. Mary took _____ coat off the hook.
2. _____ wished upon a star.
3. I want _____ to go with me.
4. The boys were playing ball with _____ .
5. One of _____ sisters drove the car.
6. The tree was taller than _____ .

Articles

D. Fill in the blanks with the correct articles.

The article "an" is used before a vowel.

1. She took a bite of _____ apple. (a, the)
2. Winston wore _____ blue suit. (a, an)
3. Stella swam in _____ lake. (an, the)
4. Lori took _____ shortcut home. (a, an)
5. May has _____ apple with bumps. (a, an)
6. Did you go to _____ mall? (the, an)

Progress Test 2

Verbs

E. Underline the "present" or "past" tense verb that fits best in each sentence.

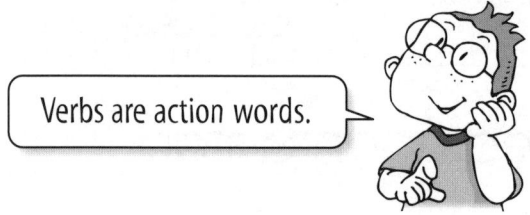

Verbs are action words.

1. She (live, lives) in a new house.
2. Frances (touch, touched) the wet paint.
3. Did you (look, looked) at the newspaper?
4. Jim (work, worked) on his car.
5. Henry (watch, watched) his favourite TV show.

F. Underline the verb in each sentence.

1. She is working at that store.
2. Marcie learned how to skate.
3. Did you climb the tree?
4. My mom cooks good food.
5. Dad is talking on the phone.
6. I can make a house of cards.
7. Will you skate on the rink?
8. Tracy makes her own clothes.

Adjectives

Remember: Adjectives are words that describe nouns.

G. Look at each picture. Write an adjective that suits the noun in the space.

| old   pretty   happy   bright |

 1. the _____ sun

2. the _____ boot

 3. the _____ flowers

4. a _____ face

H. Draw a line to match the adjective with the noun it describes.

broken   juicy   green   soft   shiny

Progress Test 2

Sentences

A sentence is a group of words that tells a complete idea.

I. Read each sentence. Put in the correct punctuation.

1. Wow, that's great _____ (. ! ?)
2. Where are you going _____ (. ! ?)
3. I have an orange _____ (. ! ?)
4. I like to watch TV _____ (. ! ?)
5. Do you want some cereal _____ (. ! ?)

The subject tells who or what the sentence is about. The predicate tells something about the subject.

J. Underline the subjects and put the predicates in parentheses ( ).

1. The boy took a bath.
2. The candle blew out.
3. Ben took the train.
4. The lamp was lit all day.
5. Mark is going to the doctor.
6. The children drew pictures on the driveway.
7. Margaret is visiting her aunt.

When you change the word order of a sentence, you can change its meaning.

The dog is bigger than the cat.
The cat is bigger than the dog.

K. Read each sentence. Change the word order to make a silly sentence.

1. A goat is larger than a chicken.
   _____

2. A house is bigger than a mouse.
   _____

3. The knife is on the counter.
   _____

4. The chair is on the floor.
   _____

5. A snake can eat a mouse.
   _____

6. A strawberry is juicier than an apple.
   _____

7. a grape is greener than a pear.
   _____

8. The CN Tower is higher than the train station.
   _____

Section 3

Vocabulary & Usage

1. The Five Senses

Human beings have five senses: touch, smell, sight, hearing, and taste. We touch with our hands. The human hand has many bones. We smell with our nose and see with our eyes. We hear with our ears and taste with our tongue.

A. Write three words that match each sense.

smell

see

hear

taste

touch

WORD BANK

fingers   nose   sweet   ears   palm
loud   lids   scent   sound   hard
nostrils   eyes   picture   tongue   sour

B. Fill in the missing letters to complete the words.

1. h __ m __ n
2. s __ e __ __
3. h __ __ r __ __ g
4. b __ __ __ s
5. h __ __ d
6. h __ __ r
7. t __ __ t __
8. t __ __ __ h

C. Draw a line to match each pair of words that rhyme.

Words that rhyme sound the same at the end.

1. bone • • tell
2. five • • ear
3. sense • • spy
4. hear • • tense
5. nose • • cone
6. eye • • rose
7. smell • • bee
8. see • • hive

D. Unscramble the letters on the hands and write the words they make.

1.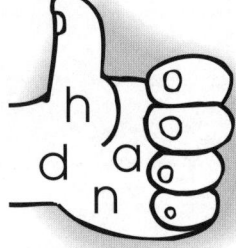

2.

3.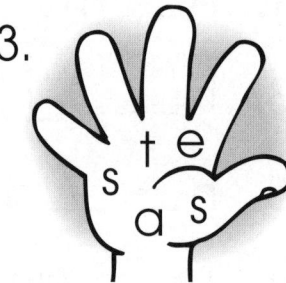

4.

5.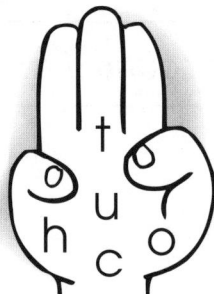

6.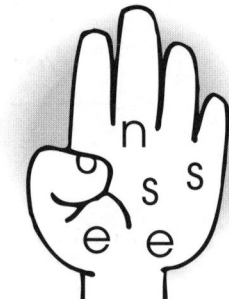

7.

8.

9.

10.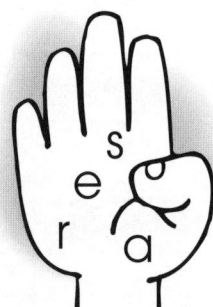

11.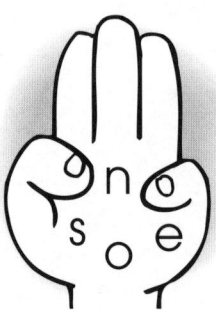

12.

E. Find the words in the word search.

k	y	d	m	s	c	u	s	i	g	h	t	b	z
x	w	t	u	g	k	m	h	e	o	d	f	h	i
b	d	o	f	j	e	c	o	k	h	q	t	s	u
p	w	n	r	v	a	f	t	o	u	c	h	w	o
d	k	g	k	u	r	i	w	y	m	b	p	v	l
a	z	u	h	l	s	q	b	g	a	o	o	m	h
s	e	e	c	p	x	u	h	a	n	d	t	f	e
y	i	t	f	v	j	a	o	l	u	y	d	x	a
g	p	s	m	e	l	l	w	q	c	j	m	i	r
k	m	o	r	y	o	y	b	i	g	b	v	l	c
t	a	s	t	e	r	t	o	z	r	o	n	r	q
h	c	u	w	s	j	v	n	o	s	e	h	m	k
w	i	p	s	e	n	s	e	b	l	f	i	v	e
n	l	b	c	r	b	f	s	h	x	p	d	t	i

Word Bank

human	five	smell	bones
tongue	hand	touch	taste
nose	hear	sight	sense
see	eyes	ears	body

2 Changing Seasons

There are four seasons in every year: Spring, Summer, Fall, and Winter.

Spring is the season when the weather gets warmer and buds come out on trees. Spring begins in March and ends in June.

Summer begins in June and ends in September. It is the season when temperatures get high. The leaves are green and the grass is too!

Fall is the season when leaves change from green to orange, yellow, red, and brown. Leaves change colour because the temperature drops.

Winter starts in December and ends in March. In Canada, there is usually a lot of snow in winter. Snow is one type of precipitation.

A. Look at the boxes. Finish the words that belong to each season.

FALL

o _ _ _ _ e
y _ _ _ _ w
_ _ _ _ n

WINTER

s _ _ _
D _ _ _ m _ _ _
pr _ _ _ _ _ _ _ _ t _ _ _

B. Join the pictures to the words.

snow
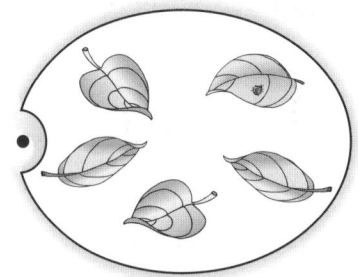

leaves

Winter

Fall

hot

Spring

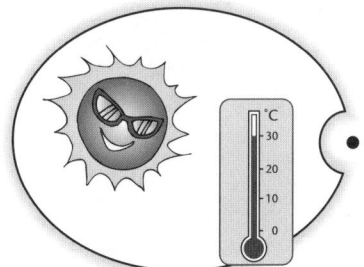
Summer
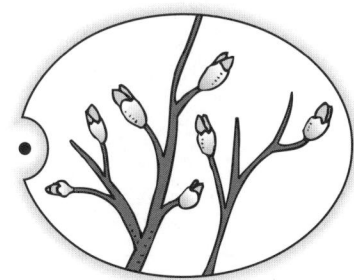

buds

2

Word Families – Rhyming Words

C. Fill in the missing letters to make words that rhyme.

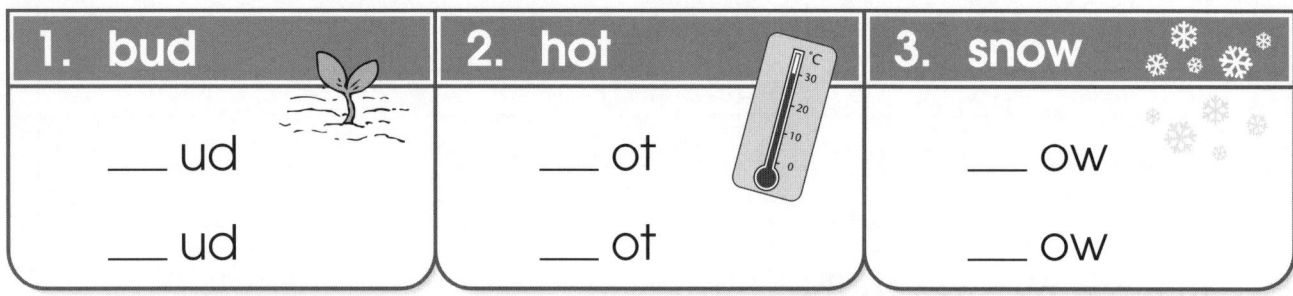

1. bud	2. hot	3. snow
__ ud	__ ot	__ ow
__ ud	__ ot	__ ow

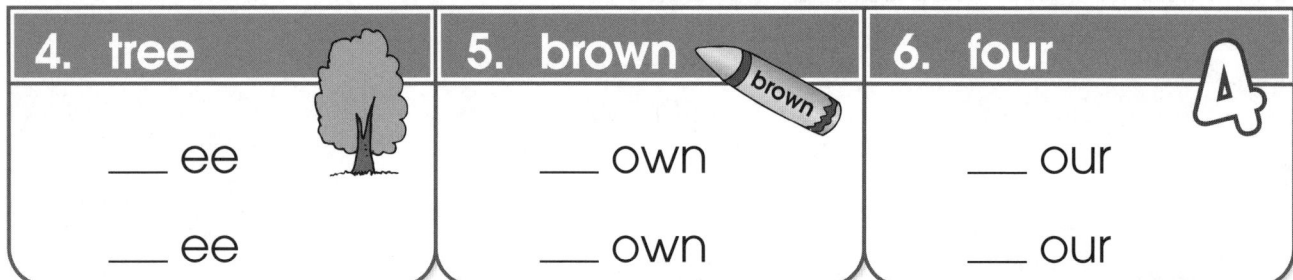

4. tree	5. brown	6. four
__ ee	__ own	__ our
__ ee	__ own	__ our

D. The words in these leaves are scrambled. Sort them and write each on the line below.

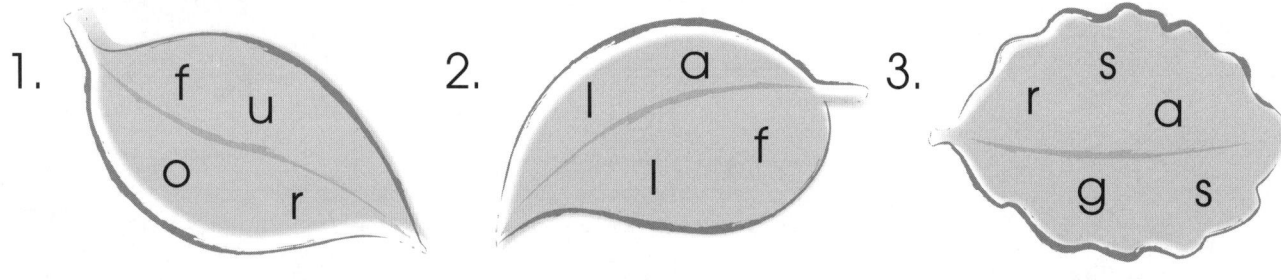

1. f, u, o, r
2. a, l, l, f
3. s, r, a, g, s

_____   _____   _____

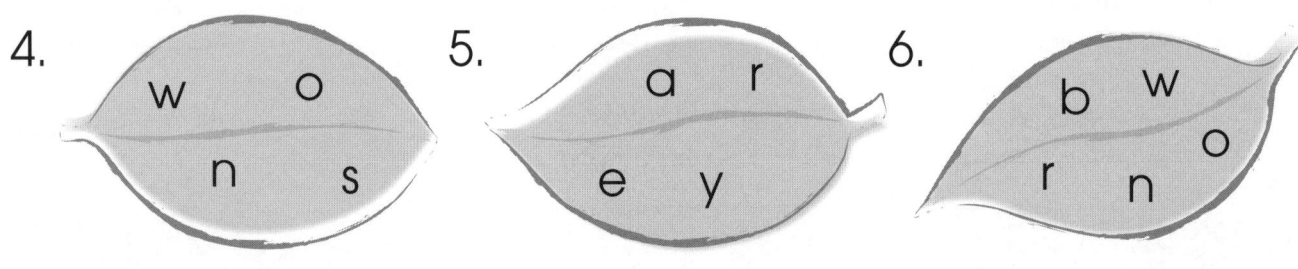

4. w, o, n, s
5. a, r, e, y
6. b, w, o, r, n

_____   _____   _____

7. 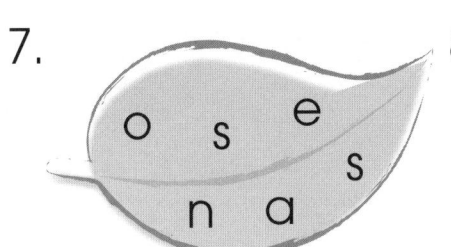 8.  9.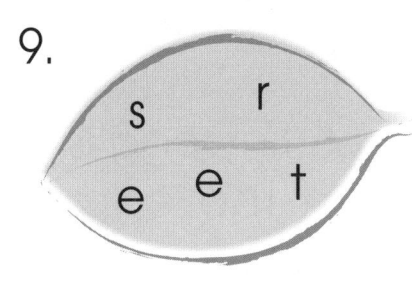

_____   _____   _____

E. **Put the words in order and write the correct sentences.**

1. | leaves | | The | | green | | are |

   _____

2. | colours | | Leaves | | many | | in | | are |

   _____

3. | four | | There | | seasons | | year | | every | | in | | are |

   _____

4. | begins | | March | | Spring | | ends | | June | | in | | and | | in |

   _____

5. | Snow | | precipitation | | is | | a | | of | | type |

   _____

6. | season | | Each | | is | | three | | months | | about | | long |

   _____

3 The Butterfly

A tiny egg is laid on a leaf. Then the egg hatches and becomes a caterpillar. The caterpillar eats and eats and becomes very fat. It forms a pupa or cover around itself.

After a few weeks, the pupa hatches and a butterfly is born. The female butterfly is not as colourful as the male.

The butterfly flies among flowers and eats nectar. Sometimes it feeds on the juices from fruits that are rotting.

A. Look at each picture. Write what it is.

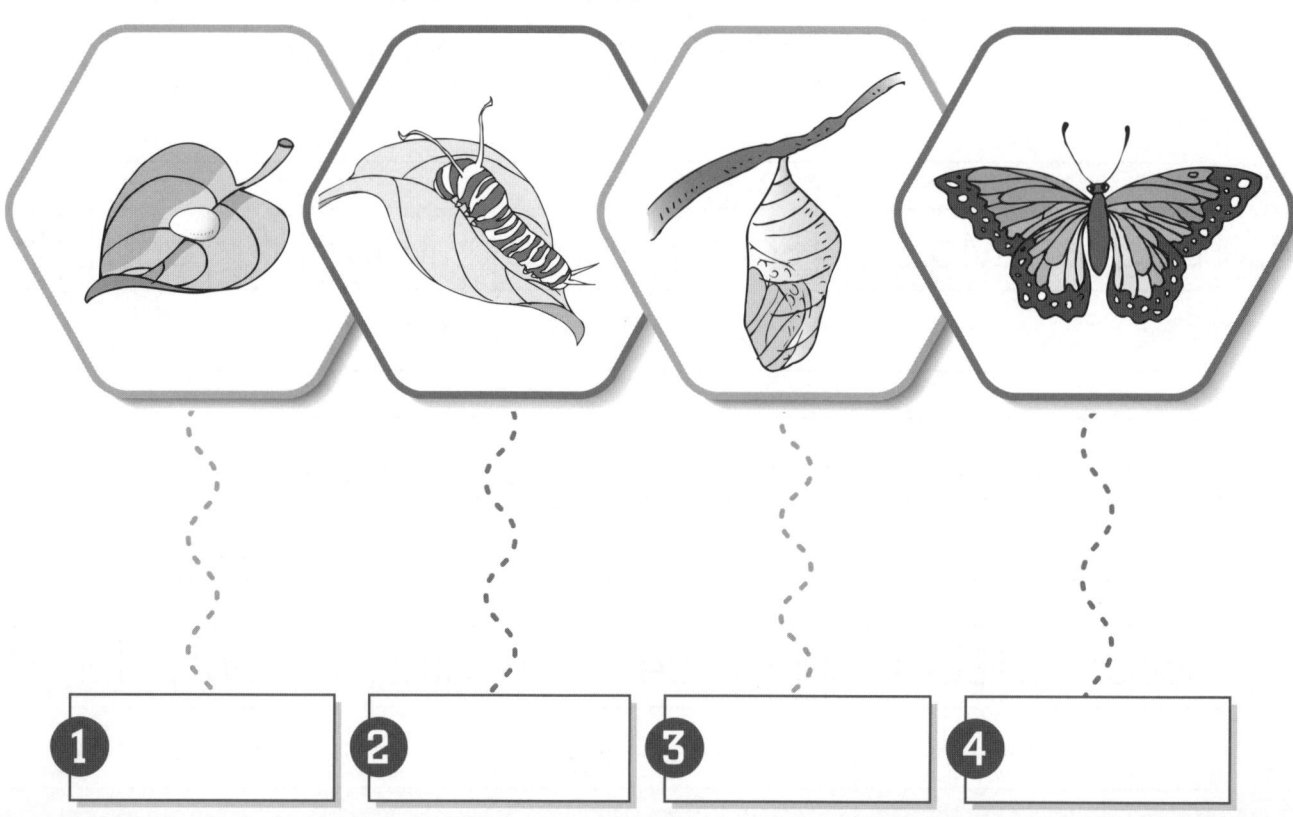

1.
2.
3.
4.

B. Draw lines to match the butterflies with the flowers to form words.

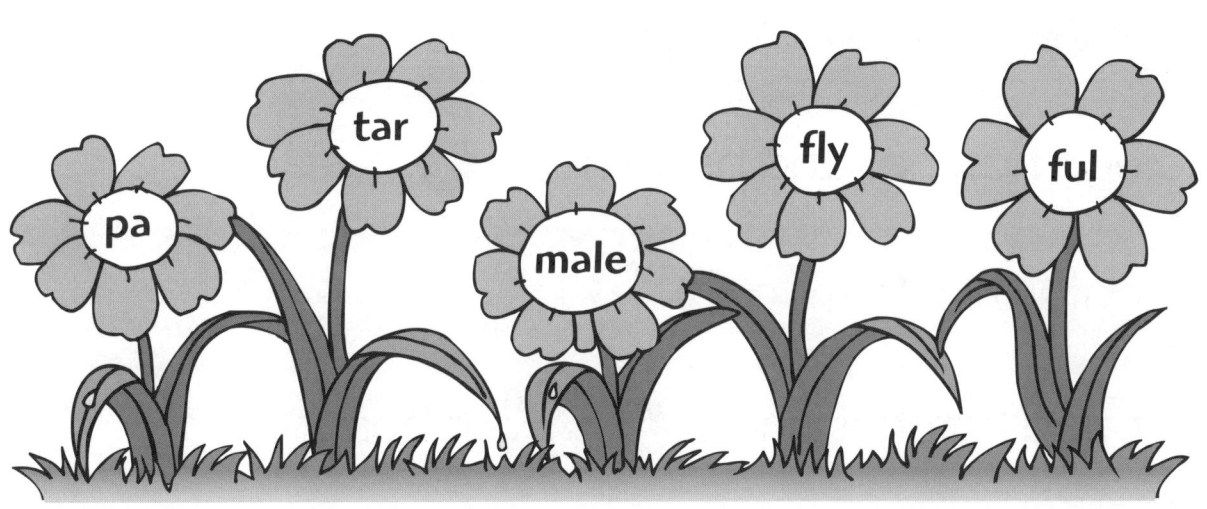

C. Read the first word in each box. Write letters in the blanks to make new words.

1. **laid**

   ___ aid

   ___ aid

2. **fat**

   ___ at

   ___ at

3. **few**

   ___ ew

   ___ ew

4. **born**

   ___ orn

   ___ orn

5. **male**

   ___ ale

   ___ ale

6. **not**

   ___ ot

   ___ ot

3

D. Read each sentence. Write a word for each picture.

WORD BANK

egg   caterpillar   butterfly   fruits
leaf   pupa   flowers

A tiny **1** is laid on a **2** .

The egg hatches and becomes a **3** 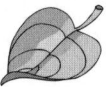 .

The caterpillar forms a **4** .

The pupa hatches and a **5**  is born.

The butterfly eats nectar from **6**  .

It also eats juices from **7**  .

1. _ _ _   2. _ _ _ _

3. _ _ _ _ _ _ _ _ _ _ _

4. _ _ _ _   5. _ _ _ _ _ _ _ _ _

6. _ _ _ _ _ _ _   7. _ _ _ _ _ _

E. Read the word. Write it in a sentence. The first one is done for you.

1. **tiny**
The eggs are tiny.

2. **laid**
_____

3. **leaf**
_____

4. **caterpillar**
_____

5. **pupa**
_____

6. **butterfly**
_____

7. **fruit**
_____

4 Crispy Squares

Amanda and her mom are making crispy squares. Maybe you would like their recipe.

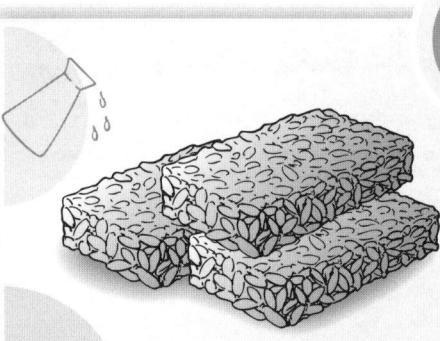

Crispy Squares

Ingredients:

- 5 cups of rice crispies
- 1 packet of small marshmallows
- $\frac{1}{2}$ cup of margarine

Utensils:

- 1 large bowl
- 1 saucepan
- 1 spatula
- 1 large glass baking dish
- measuring spoons

Directions :

Melt margarine in saucepan. Pour in marshmallows slowly and keep stirring until marshmallows are melted. Take marshmallow mixture from stove. Mix in large bowl with rice crispies.

Pat into large, greased baking dish. Cool in refrigerator. Cut into squares.

A. Read the letters inside each crispy square. Unscramble to make a word.

1. erci
2. blwo
3. spuc
4. ciyrsp
5. orpu
6. toevs
7. noosps
8. kabing
9. hisd
10. qussera
11. napseacu
12. retxium

4

In baking, it is important to follow directions in the correct order. This is true for many other activities.

B. Read these directions. Put them in the correct order.

a) Mix eggs and milk together.
Take the ingredients out of the fridge.
Pour pancake batter onto a frying pan.
Pour in flour and baking powder.

1. _____
2. _____
3. _____
4. _____

b) Blow up the balloon.
Twist the opening to make a knot.
Take a balloon out of the package.
Buy a package of balloons.

1. _____
2. _____
3. _____
4. _____

C. Look at each picture. Write a sentence about what is happening.

1

2

3

4

5 Nunavut

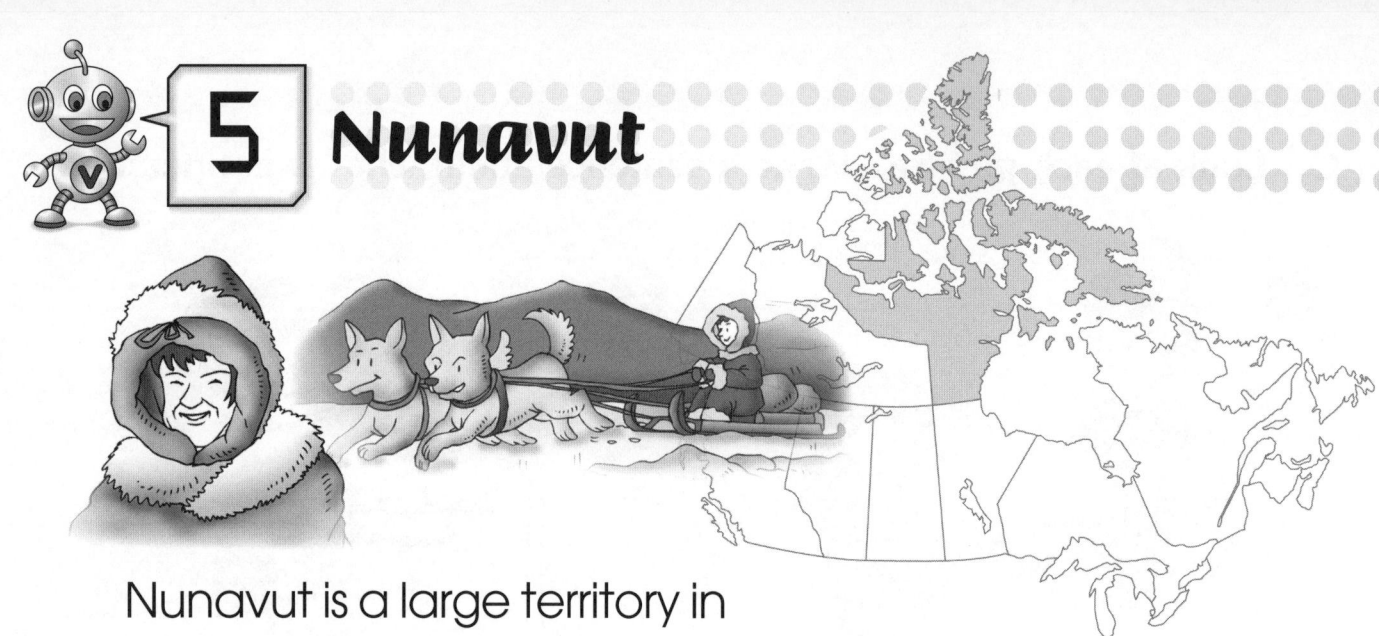

Nunavut is a large territory in the north of Canada. It is near the North Pole. It is very cold there. Not many plants grow there because it is so cold.

In Nunavut, there are six months of darkness and six months of daylight. You might see the sun shining at 9 o'clock at night in June.

Would you like to go to bed when the sun is shining and go to school when it is dark outside?

A. Read the sentences. Find the missing words from the passage.

The last two are for you to figure out.

1. Nunavut is a _____ in Canada.

2. Nunavut is near the _____ _____ .

3. In Nunavut, there are _____ months of darkness.

4. The sun might be shining at _____ in June.

5. Not many _____ grow in Nunavut.

6. Plants don't grow because it is very _____ .

7. In the cold weather, people wear warm _____ .

8. Some people in Nunavut ride on _____ .

B. Sort out the letters in the igloos to make new words.

1.
 _____

2.
 _____

3. _____

4.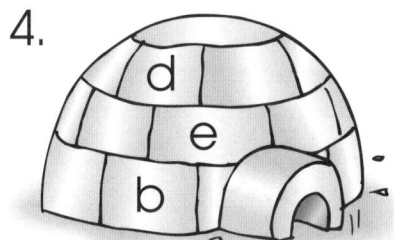
 _____

5.
 _____

6.
 _____

7.
 _____

8.
 _____

9.
 _____

10.
 _____

11.
 _____

12. _____

5

Sometimes you can find smaller words inside large ones.

C. Read each word. Find the smaller word and write it on the lines below. The first one is done for you.

1. north n o r	2. Canada _ _ _	3. near _ _ _
4. cold _ _ _	5. there _ _ _	6. not _ _
7. many _ _ _	8. plants _ _ _ _	9. grow _ _ _
10. there _ _ _ _	11. darkness _ _ _ _	12. daylight _ _ _
13. daylight _ _ _	14. outside _ _ _	15. outside _ _ _ _

Challenge

Try one of your own!

_____ (large word)

_____ (small word)

D. **Use these words in sentences.**

1. large

   _____

   _____

2. north

   _____

   _____

3. cold

   _____

   _____

4. plants

   _____

   _____

5. months

   _____

   _____

6. school

   _____

   _____

7. dark

   _____

   _____

6 Word Fun

Poetry – Alphabet Rhymes

A is for apple.

B is for <u>bog</u>.

C is for cat and

D is for <u>dog</u>.

E is for egg.

F is for <u>fat</u>.

G is for game and

H is for <u>hat</u>.

Did you notice that the last words in the second and fourth lines rhyme or sound the same?

A. **Make up an alphabet rhyme of your own. Fill in the blanks with rhyming words.**

I is for icicle.

J is for 1._____.

K is for kite and

L is for 3._____.

M is for moose.

N is for 2._____.

O is for otter and

P is for 4._____.

B. **Read the clues and complete the word puzzle.**

Across

A. An animal that lives in water and rhymes with "potter"
B. It slithers and rhymes with "cake".
C. This animal is afraid of cats but rhymes with "cat".
D. A fat animal that rhymes with "wig"

Down

1. A woolly animal that rhymes with "deep"
2. A huge sea animal that rhymes with "tale"
3. An animal that rhymes with "goose"
4. A big cat with stripes
5. A big animal that rhymes with "pear"
6. A frog-like animal that rhymes with "road"

C. **Write a word that sounds the same as the underlined word in each sentence.**

1. The <u>ad</u> was for chocolate chip cookies.

   Can you _____ 35 and 23?

2. The trees are <u>bare</u> in winter.

   The _____ climbed the tree.

3. The wind <u>blew</u> over the water.

   The water and sky are _____ .

4. Emily walked <u>by</u> the house.

   She wants to _____ a new dress.

5. <u>I</u> hope to go to the city.

   Did you hurt your _____ ?

6. Mom likes the <u>red</u> roses.

   I _____ a funny story last night.

7. Mom used the <u>flour</u> to make cookies.

   I picked a _____ to give to my mom.

Acrostic Poetry

Acrostic poems have one word that goes ↓. Each letter is the first letter of a new word. All the words might belong to the first word in some way.

D. Use these words to write acrostic poems.

1. **D** _____
   O _____
   G _____

2. **H** _____
   A _____
   T _____

3. **B** _____
   A _____
   L _____
   L _____

E. Using words you like, write an acrostic poem of your own. Draw a picture to go with it.

7 What Makes a Fish a Fish?

Fish live in ponds, streams, lakes, and oceans. Some fish are kept as pets in fishbowls and aquariums.

Fish swim by moving their tails and waving their fins.

All fish have backbones. Most fish have skin that is covered with scales. Scales protect the skin from cuts and scrapes. There is slime over the scales to protect the fish from germs in the water.

Fish have gills for breathing. Most fish eat tiny plants or tiny animals like worms.

Word Family – Rhyming Words

A. Look at each word. Fill in the letters that make rhyming words.

1. fin
__ in
__ in

2. pet
__ et
__ et

3. gill
__ ill
__ ill

4. tail
__ ail
__ ail

5. fish
__ ish
__ ish

6. lake
__ ake
__ ake

B. Each of these sentences has a word that is not spelled correctly. Cross out the word and write the correct spelling in the box. Use the word bank to help you.

there *eat* *oceans* *wave*
scales *streams* *tails* *aquariums*

1. Codfish live in oseans.

[ ]

2. All fish have backbones and tales.

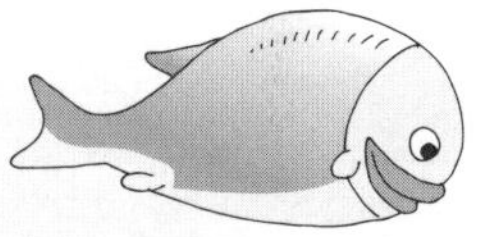

[ ]

3. Most fish also have scails.

[ ]

4. Fish waive their fins to help them swim.

[ ]

5. Most fish eet tiny plants.

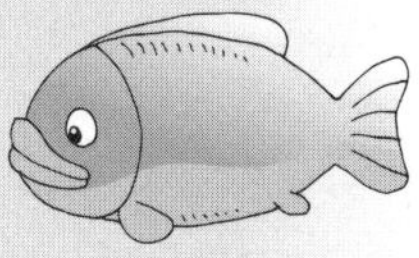

[ ]

6. Their are many species of fish.

[ ]

7. Some fish live in steams.

[ ]

8. Some fish are kept in aguariums.

[ ]

C. The words on the fish are jumbled. Sort them out and write them as sentences.

1. live oceans Fish and in ponds .

2. swim moving Fish by tails . their

3. fish All backbones have .

4. help . Gills to fish breathe

5. protect Scales fish's the skin .

6. make pets . Some good fish

D. Make a sentence with each of these words.

1. live
   _____

2. fishbowl
   _____

3. ocean
   _____

4. pet
   _____

5. swim
   _____

6. tail
   _____

Use these two words to write a sentence.

_____

_____

PROGRESS TEST 1

A. Unscramble the letters to make words.

1. x b o
   _____

2. p c u
   _____

3. c s k o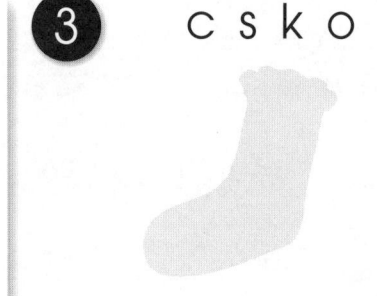
   _____

4. t a b
   _____

5. c e k a
   _____

6. k i l m
   _____

7. s e g o o
   _____

8. p a m l
   _____

9. l f e a
   _____

10. s l a c e s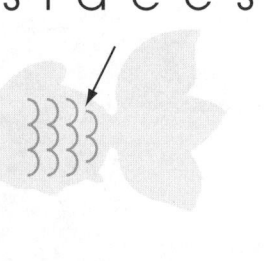
    _____

11. i s n c e t
    _____

12. l l i g
    _____

B. Find the small word hidden inside each of these larger words.

1. flat — fat
2. stop — _____
3. spot — _____
4. tart — _____
5. pear — _____
6. treat — _____
7. witch — _____
8. person — _____
9. summer — _____
10. cold — _____
11. sand — _____
12. fish — _____
13. tray — _____
14. season — _____
15. four — _____
16. cookie — _____
17. warm — _____
18. plant — _____

PROGRESS TEST 1

C. Put the words in the correct order to make sentences.

Don't forget to begin a sentence with a capital letter and put a period at the end of it.

1. computer   plays   Mike   his   with

   _____

 2. Amanda   pool   in   swims   her

   _____

3. are   there   books   four   table   on   the

   _____

 4. the   today   is   sun   hot

   _____

5. Caitlin   shoes   red   has   of   a   pair

   _____

 6. dark   bats   look   food   in   the   for

   _____

D. Read each sentence. Fill in the blank with a verb that makes sense.

driving licking riding sucking
skates plays paints
danced watered cut

1. Cathy _____ at the arena.

2. Bill _____ the room green.

3. Is your dad _____ you to school?

4. How many girls are _____ their bikes?

5. Jason _____ baseball well.

6. The cat is _____ her paw.

7. Janet _____ the plants yesterday.

8. The baby boy is _____ his thumb.

9. Clare _____ the apple in half.

10. We _____ to the music.

PROGRESS TEST 1

E. Each sentence below has a word that sounds right but is not spelled correctly. Cross out the wrong word and write the correct one on the line below.

> mail   ate   played   made   sail
> trade   too   flower

1. The boat set sale on the lake.
   _____

2. Rob plaid games with his friends.
   _____

3. She maid a new recipe.
   _____

4. Did you trayed the hockey card?
   _____

5. Tom eight his lunch quickly.
   _____

6. The letter arrived with the male.
   _____

7. I want to go two.
   _____

8. This flour is beautiful.
   _____

F. The first word in each set is given. Find letters that will make the words in that set.

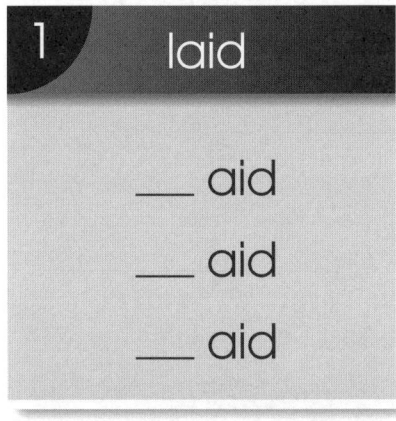

1 laid

___ aid
___ aid
___ aid

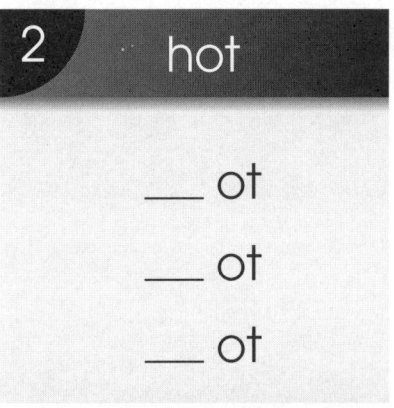

2 hot

___ ot
___ ot
___ ot

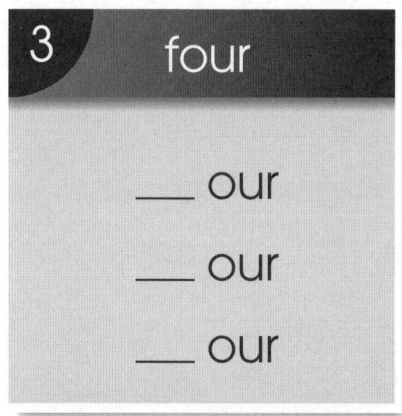

3 four

___ our
___ our
___ our

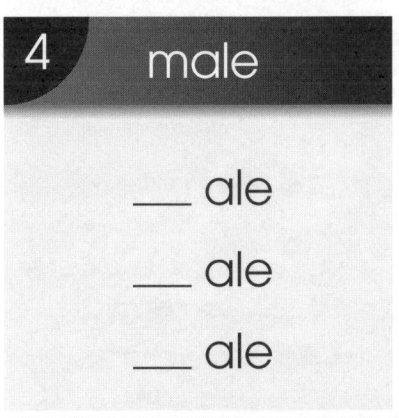

4 male

___ ale
___ ale
___ ale

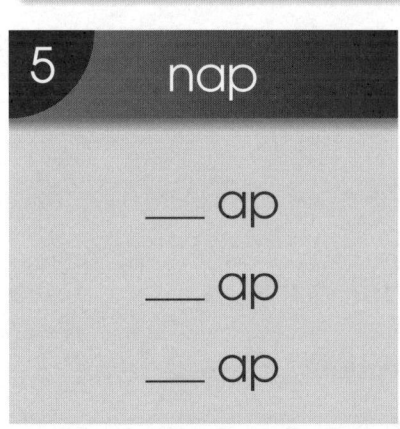

5 nap

___ ap
___ ap
___ ap

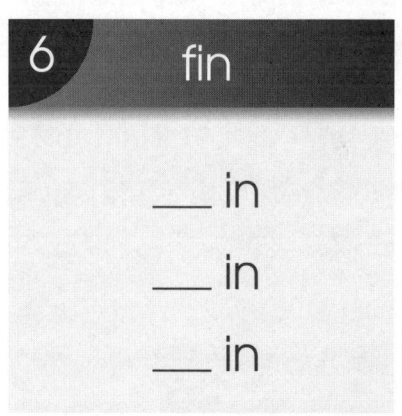

6 fin

___ in
___ in
___ in

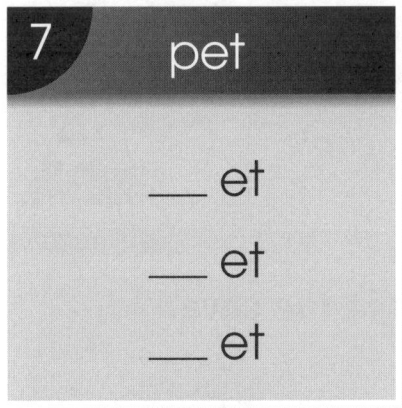

7 pet

___ et
___ et
___ et

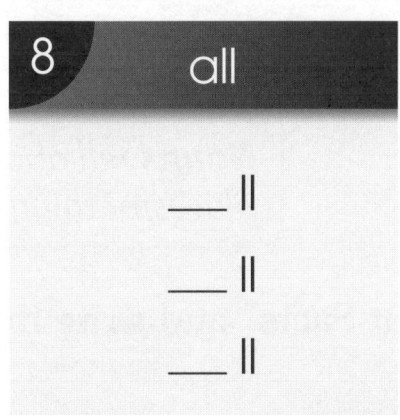

8 all

___ ll
___ ll
___ ll

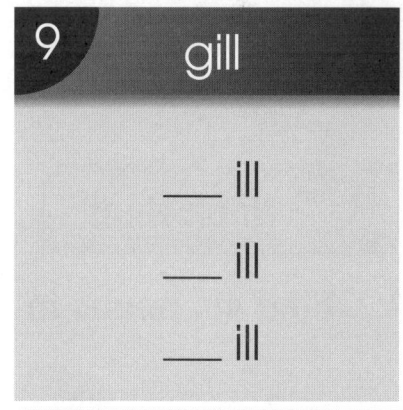

9 gill

___ ill
___ ill
___ ill

10 lake

___ ake
___ ake
___ ake

11 bail

___ ail
___ ail
___ ail

12 bear

___ ear
___ ear
___ ear

8 Bat Facts

Bats live in almost every country in the world. They do not live in places where it is very hot or very cold.

Bats usually eat fruits or insects. Vampire bats eat the blood of dead birds and cattle.

Bats have good hearing, which helps them to find food. They see best in the dark, which is when they hunt for food.

Bats are useful to farmers because they eat insects and spread seeds.

Nouns tell about people, places, or things.

A. Find six nouns in "Bat Facts" and write them in the cave.

B. Read the clues and complete the word puzzles.

Across	Down
1. You use it to hit the baseball.	A. You wear it on your head.
2. This animal mews.	B. You do this to your pet.
3. It lays on the floor.	C. This small animal has a long tail and sharp teeth.

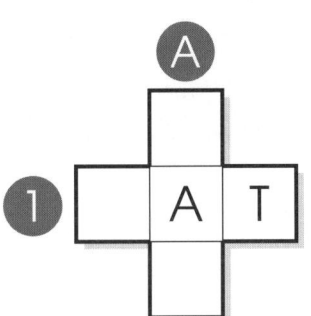 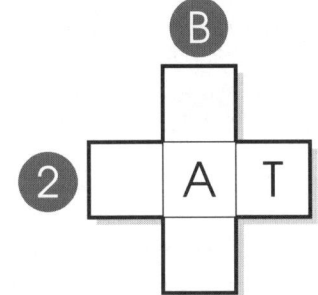 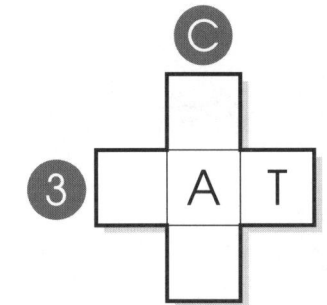

All the words in these 3 puzzles end with "at".

Across	Down
1. Things we eat	A. It has five toes.
2. We use it to build houses.	B. We can see it at night.
3. Midday	C. This is for our head.

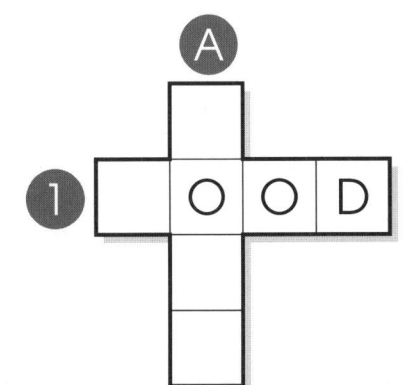 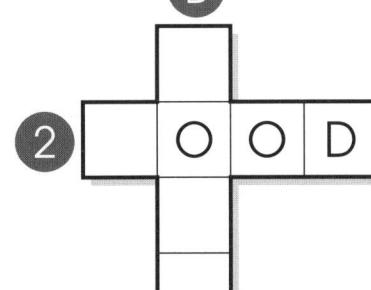 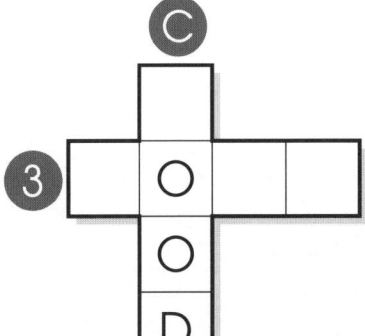

Writing Time

C. Use each of these words in a sentence.

> bats   fruit   hearing   seeds
> farmers   world   insect   food

Remember that a sentence begins with a capital letter and ends with a period.

1. _____
2. _____
3. _____
4. _____
5. _____
6. _____
7. _____
8. _____

D. The pictures below are describing the sentences in "Bat Facts". Write a sentence that tells about the picture.

1. _____
   _____
   _____
   _____

2. _____
   _____
   _____
   _____

3. _____
   _____
   _____
   _____

9 The Emperor Penguin

The Emperor Penguin is the largest of all penguins. It is about 1.2 metres tall. That's probably taller than you! It has black and grey feathers and yellow ear patches.

The Emperor Penguin lives in the Antarctic. It lives near water, never on dry land. Its food comes from the ocean, mostly fish and krill, which are like shrimp.

When the mother penguin lays the egg, she goes off to hunt for food. The father Emperor hatches the egg under a flap of skin on top of his feet.

Word Hunt

A. The words below are found in "The Emperor Penguin". Fill in the missing letters.

1. p _ _ g _ _ n
2. _ mp _ r _ r
3. A _ t _ _ c _ i _
4. k _ _ _ _ l
5. h _ _ ch _ s
6. p _ t _ h _ s
7. b _ _ ck
8. y _ l _ o _
9. t _ ll _ r
10. g _ e _

B. Read the letters on each ice floe. Sort out the letters and write the word.

1. large

2. penguin

3. feathers

4. ocean

5. shrimp

6. feather

C. **Sort the words to make sentences.**

1. Antarctica . The lives Emperor in Penguin

2. lives water land . It near dry never on ,

3. food Penguins their get the from ocean .

4. for are food Fish penguins krill and .

5. largest of the The Emperor is penguins .

6. penguin The hunts food . for mother

7. father hatches egg The the Emperor .

D. In each group of sentences, there is one that does not belong. Draw a line through the sentence that does not belong.

Example: The fly flew into the house. It landed on the stove and the table. ~~The tree is near the house.~~

1.

   ### Candy
   I love all kinds of candies. ~~Fish is not my favourite food.~~ My favourite candies are gummy bears.

2.

   ### My Bike
   I have a new bike. It is red and white. ~~The car goes in the garage.~~ My bike stays in the storage shed.

3.

   ### Amanda's Pool
   Amanda loves to swim in her pool. She asks her friends to come for a swim. ~~The flowers grow tall.~~ Her friends like to swim too.

4.

   ### T.V. Shows
   Some of the best T.V. shows I like are really funny. They make me laugh and laugh. ~~My mom likes to dance.~~

10 Playing Soccer

Today I started soccer. I went to a big field where there were lots of children the same age as I. They all had the same orange uniforms too!

My soccer coach is named Olivia. She is really nice and friendly. She said, "Hello, my name is Olivia." Then she told us that we would practise twice a week and play games. She said the most important thing was to have fun.

A. Look at the pictures. Write what you think each person is saying.

B. Read the "describing" words in Column A and draw a line to match each one with a word in Column B.

	Column A			Column B
1.	tall	•	•	ladybug
2.	green	•	•	ball
3.	tiny	•	•	knife
4.	blue	•	•	girl
5.	round	•	•	tree
6.	sharp	•	•	grass
7.	pretty	•	•	candy
8.	sweet	•	•	sky
9.	rainy	•	•	game
10.	fun	•	•	day

C. Read each of these sentences. Colour the word that has the same meaning as the underlined word.

1. I put the small seed in the jar.

   | tiny | | green |

2. Mike found a giant zucchini in the garden.

   | long | | huge |

3. Theo kicked the soccer ball two times.

   | twice | | thrice |

4. There is a very high building in the city.

   | big | | tall |

5. There were several people waiting.

   | a few | | many |

6. There were forty thieves in the story.

   | robbers | | friends |

7. Becca ran quickly to the end of the field.

   | fast | | slowly |

D. **Fill in the blanks with words from the passage.**

Today I started 1._____ . I went to a 2._____ where there were lots of 3._____ . They were the same 4._____ as I. We all had orange 5._____ .

Olivia is our 6._____ . She is nice and 7._____ . She said that we would 8._____ twice a week and play 9._____ . She told us to have 10._____ .

Write three sentences about our coach, Olivia.

1. _____
2. _____
3. _____

11 Ladybugs

Ladybugs are insects. They are often red with black spots. Some are black with red spots. In summer, they live on flowers, shrubs, and in fields. In winter, they live in trees and houses.

Ladybugs are useful because they eat the insects that kill plants. These insects are called aphides. Ladybugs eat over 5,000 aphides in a lifetime.

Ladybugs have some enemies. They are called parasites and they eat the inside of the ladybug. Human beings are also their enemies because they spray them with poison and disturb their nests and homes.

Rhyming Pairs

Rhyming words sound the same at the end.

A. Write a rhyming word to match each word below.

1. nest ___ est
2. spot ___ ot
3. bug ___ ug
4. that ___ at
5. black ___ ack
6. live ___ ive
7. kill ___ ill
8. some ___ ome

B. Draw a line to join each of the words with its meaning.

1. ladybug • • mess up

2. aphid • • a place where birds live

3. parasites • • an insect that eats plants and is eaten by ladybugs

4. enemy • • a bright colour

5. poison • • a bug that is red and black

6. nest • • low green bushes

7. disturb • • someone or something that kills ladybugs

8. shrubs • • They eat the inside of ladybugs.

9. red • • a spray to kill insects

10. spots • • dots

C. Draw a line to join each ladybug with a flower to make a word. Write the words on the lines.

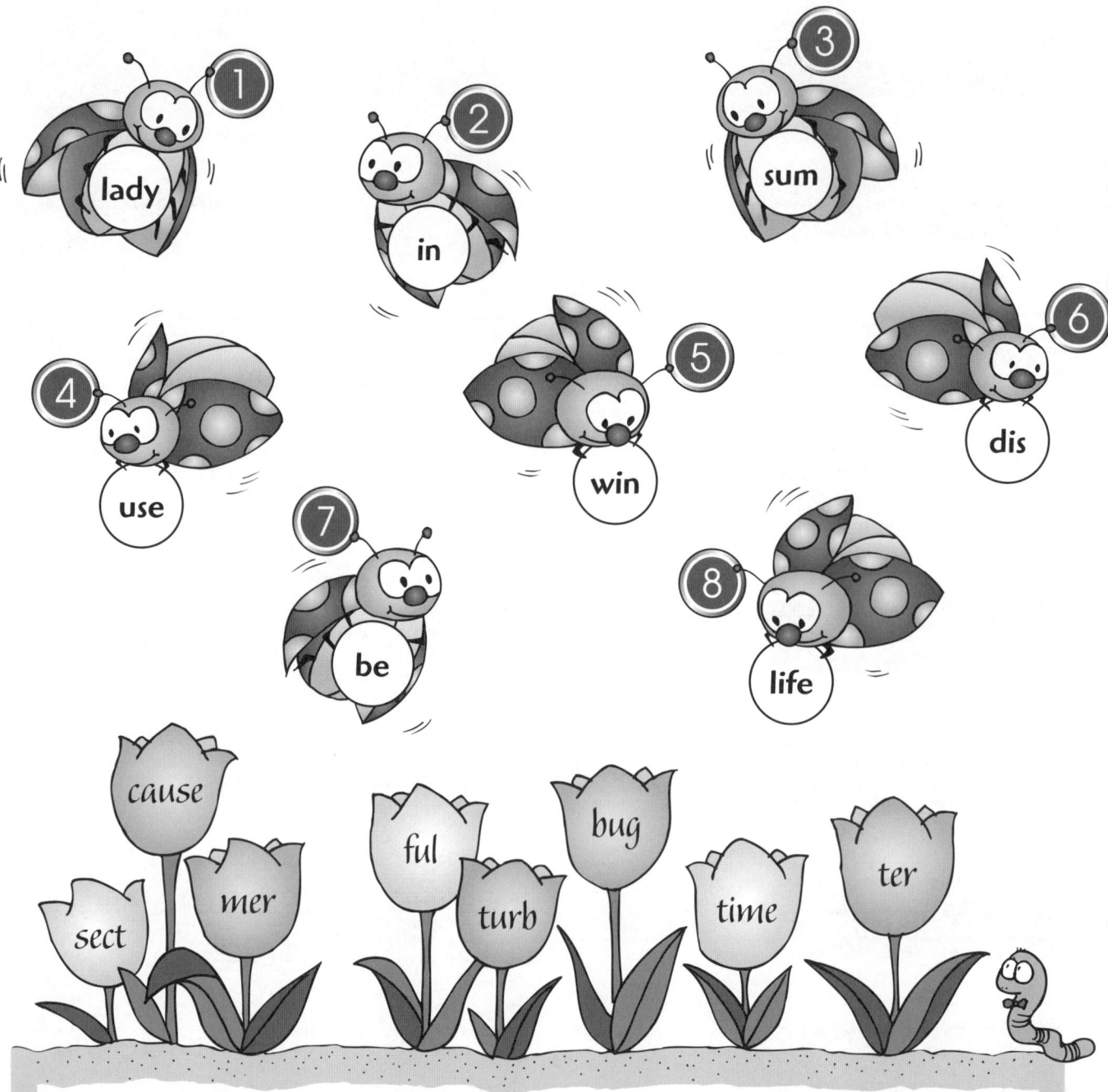

1. _____ 2. _____
3. _____ 4. _____
5. _____ 6. _____
7. _____ 8. _____

D. **Unscramble the sentences.**

Remember to begin a sentence with a capital letter and put a period at the end of it.

1. are black ladybugs red and

   _____

2. live shrubs they flowers in and

   _____

3. winter they in houses trees and in live

   _____

4. useful are ladybugs eat insects because they

   _____

5. are aphides that insects eat ladybugs

   _____

6. enemies some ladybugs have

   _____

7. are enemies human beings the of ladybugs also

   _____

12 The New Umbrella

Mom bought me a new umbrella. It is red, blue, and yellow. It looks really neat when you twirl around the handle.

I can use my umbrella in the rain and also in the sun. It protects me from the rain and from getting a sunburn.

My mom told me that the first umbrella was used about 3,000 years ago in Egypt. In more modern times, the first umbrella was used for rain in Scotland in the 1800's.

Making New Words

A. There are smaller words that can come out of larger ones. Find the small word in the larger one.

1. yellow
2. when
3. also

4. rain
5. that
6. told

7. sunburn
8. neat
9. years

10. about
11. more
12. was

B. Find these words in the word search. Circle the words.

umbrella   Scotland   years
blue   twirl   time   red   sunburn
neat   yellow   modern   really   handle
protect   Egypt   rain   new

e	r	t	y	a	j	m	r	y	u	d	e	m	v	t	y
c	n	k	i	g	r	n	o	e	f	i	S	e	d	e	w
t	i	u	m	b	r	e	l	l	a	e	c	l	o	f	g
w	a	n	E	y	e	w	o	l	y	m	o	d	e	r	n
p	l	i	g	a	d	m	n	o	w	a	t	f	a	r	d
h	S	o	q	r	b	o	t	w	i	r	l	d	E	o	r
l	a	z	s	q	u	i	b	r	h	i	a	e	x	p	m
d	l	o	u	w	b	q	u	v	o	p	n	m	s	q	y
w	h	a	n	d	l	e	r	m	E	f	d	b	e	u	o
y	n	i	b	w	u	w	i	i	g	r	n	a	s	x	u
e	d	t	u	r	e	a	l	l	y	w	e	d	r	j	E
a	m	t	r	u	m	b	p	w	p	t	d	w	i	o	n
r	a	i	n	s	d	p	r	o	t	e	c	t	o	y	b
s	k	m	u	d	e	a	b	s	e	m	b	i	v	f	w
y	n	e	a	t	r	w	a	e	k	i	u	t	a	S	b

C. Put the words in the correct order to make sentences.

Always begin a sentence with a capital letter and put a period at the end of it.

1. is new umbrella my colourful

   _____

2. umbrella not big too my is

   _____

3. fun is it twirl the umbrella to

   _____

4. first umbrella the Egypt in used was

   _____

5. protects me the umbrella the sun from

   _____

6. used were in Scotland umbrellas in 1800's the

   _____

7. use I the rain umbrella my in

   _____

D. Read each group of sentences. Find the sentence that does not belong and cross it out.

1. My mom bought me an umbrella. It was a present for my seventh birthday. It is red, blue, and yellow. It looks really neat. ~~My mom made me a huge birthday cake.~~

2. I have a new umbrella. It is colourful. ~~It was cloudy yesterday.~~ I can use it in the rain and also in the sun.

3. My neighbour, Jenny, has an umbrella hat. It is an umbrella but it is also a hat. She wears it on her head. ~~We often play together after school.~~ She looks cute in her umbrella hat.

E. Draw a picture of a present that you received. Write three sentences about it.

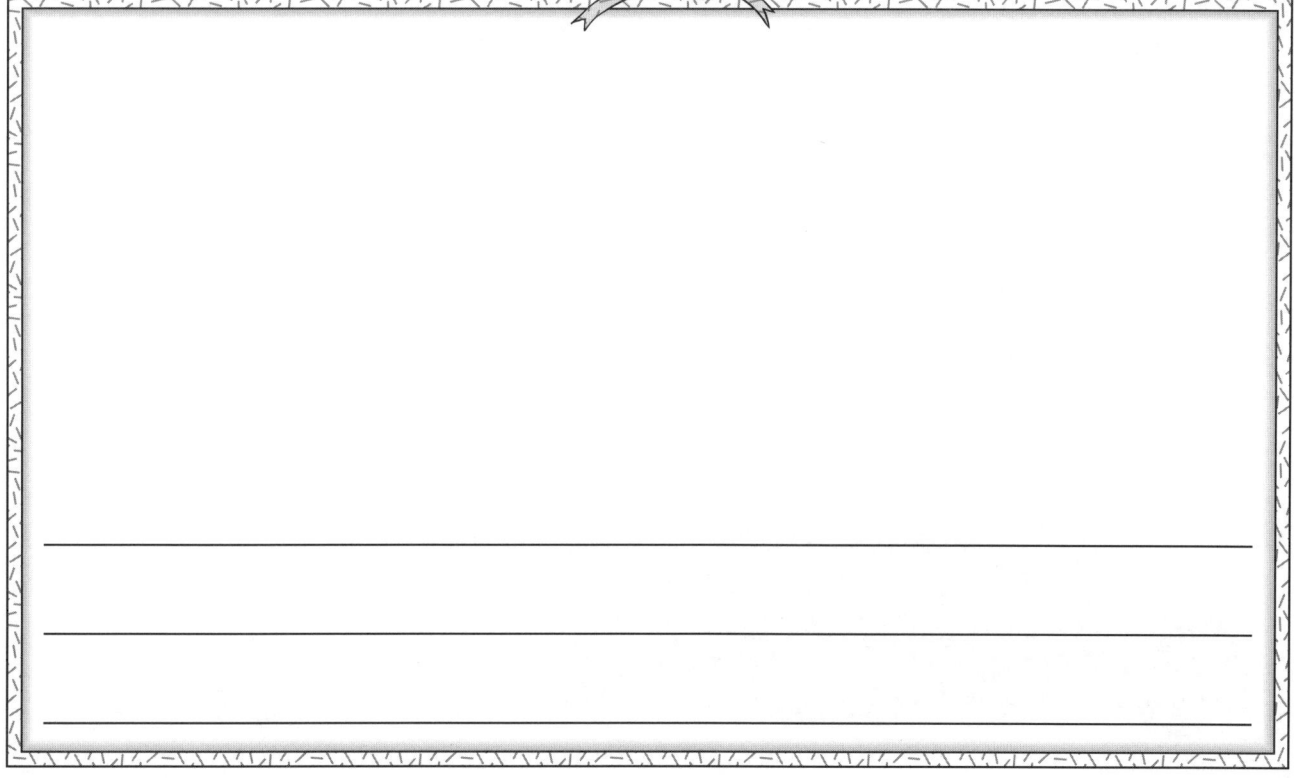

13 Sam the Firefighter

Sam is a firefighter. He works at a station near my house. Sam and his friends fight fires, but they also do a lot of other work.

At the fire station, Sam works hard to make sure that all the equipment is clean and working well. There is a lot of equipment used by firefighters, like hoses and axes.

When Sam is on duty, he stays at the fire station for many hours at a time, sometimes overnight.

A. Find these words in the passage above. Some letters have been given to you.

1. f __ r __ f __ g __ t __ r
2. __ o __ k __
3. s __ a __ i __ n
4. e q __ i __ m __ n __
5. f __ i __ n __ s
6. d __ t __
7. h __ u __ s
8. h __ s __ s
9. h __ u __ e
10. c __ e __ n
11. s __ m __ t __ m __ s
12. o __ e __ n __ g __ t

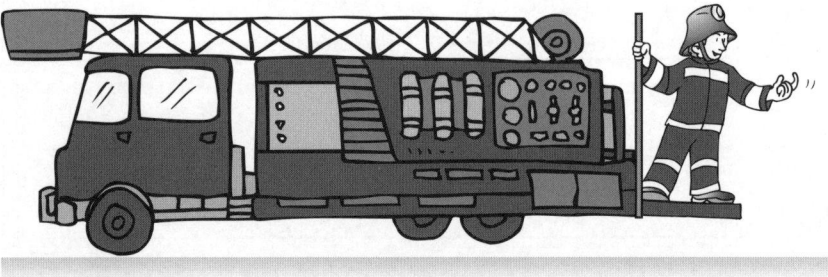

B. **In each of the following passages, there is a sentence that does not belong. Find the sentence that does not belong and draw a line through it.**

1. There were lots of bluejays in the garden. They were eating seeds and sitting on tree branches. We had lunch there.

2. Sunflowers can grow almost as tall as a one-storey house. The apple is tasty. Even the sunflower seeds are pretty big.

3. William has a new red bike. He can ride it without training wheels. His sister has a toothache.

4. Jane liked the flowers. She went to school. She picked some flowers for her dad.

5. Vincent ran all the way to the park. He played on the monkey bars. William went shopping with his mom.

6. There are seven days in every week. Sunday is the first day of the week. I enjoyed the show. Saturday is the last day.

7. Our car was dirty. We went to the carwash yesterday. There are little flies in the bushes. Now the car is clean and shiny.

13

C. Read each sentence. Cross out ✗ the incorrect word.

> Words that sound the same but have different meanings are called **homonyms**.

1. We (ate   eight) the corn.

2. The (bare   bear) lives in the woods.

3. Mary walked (buy   by) the car.

4. It takes 100 (cents   sense) to make $1.

5. The doctor checks my (wait   weight).

6. The girls took (sum   some) nuts.

7. Can you (hear   here) the music?

8. She (knew   new) the answer.

9. Judy picked the (flower   flour).

10. Will she (cell   sell) the candy to me?

11. I got stung by a (be   bee)!

12. The police (caught   court) the thieves.

D. These pictures tell about firefighters. Write a sentence about what is happening in each picture. You may use the words in the Word Bank to help you.

WORD BANK

firefighters   fight   fire truck
fire   pole   slide   hose

1. _____
_____
_____

2. _____
_____
_____

3. _____
_____
_____

4. _____
_____
_____

14 The Cactus

The cactus plant grows in the desert where it is hot in the day and cold at night. There is very little rainfall in the desert. When it does rain, the shallow roots soak up rainwater quickly. The leaves of the cactus plant are fat and thick. They can expand to hold the water. This means that the plant still has water even when it does not rain for a long period of time.

Rebus Stories

Rebus means using pictures to take the place of words.

Example: sun

A. Choose two sentences in the story and write them in rebus form.

The 🌵 plant grows in the 〜 where it is very hot in the ☀ and cold at ☁.

1. _____

2. _____

B. Each of the sentences below has a misspelled word. Circle the misspelled word and write the correct spelling in the box.

1. The cactus plant grows in the dessert.

2. It also has shellow roots.

3. The cactas plant has thick leaves.

4. There is no rain for a long peried of time.

5. The leaves expend to hold water.

6. The water gets stord in the leaves.

7. The leaves are fat and think.

8. There is little ranefall.

C. Each of these sentences has a word that does not make sense. Find a word that fits and write it above the one that doesn't.

Example: In the desert, it is ~~cold~~ hot in the day.

1. In the desert, it is hot at night.

2. There is very much rainfall.

3. In the desert, it does not rain for a short period of time.

4. The cactus roots soak up rainwater slowly.

5. The cactus leaves are thin.

6. The cactus leaves shrink to hold water.

7. The roots of the cactus are thick.

D. Finish the sentences. You may use your own words.

The cactus plant   ...grows in the desert.

1. A desert is _____ .

2. A cactus plant has _____ .

3. There is little _____ .

4. The cactus roots _____ .

5. The cactus leaves _____ .

6. Water is stored _____ .

7. The days in the desert _____ .

8. The nights in the desert _____ .

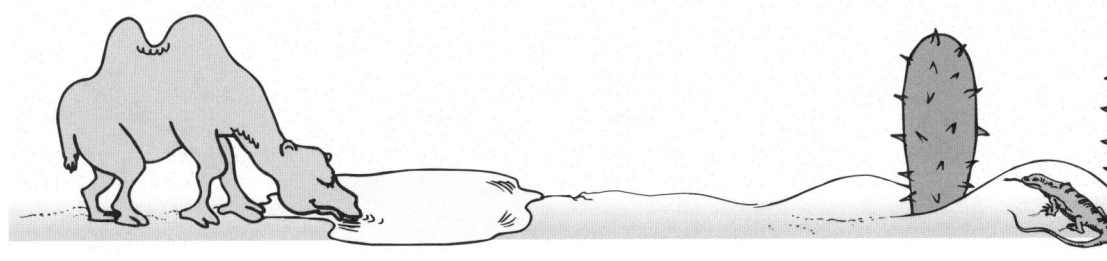

15 Marineland

Marineland is an adventure park near Niagara Falls, Canada. It has many whales and dolphins. They perform tricks like eating food from your hand. The dolphins "talk" by making special noises.

Marineland is such a great place to spend a day. Besides the sea animals at Marineland, there are also lots of rides. The roller-coaster ride is the most exciting. There are also games to play and souvenirs to buy. You can buy lots of different kinds of foods too.

Marineland is so much fun!

A. Unscramble the sentences.

Marineland | Canada | Niagara Falls | , | in | is | .

1. Marineland is in Niagara Falls, Canada.

There | animals | sea | are | there | .

2. There are sea animals there.

fun | so | There | in | Marineland | much | is | .

3. There is so much fun in Marineland.

rides | exciting | Roller-coaster | are | very | .

4. Roller-coaster rides are very exciting.

B. Complete the crossword puzzle.

Across

A. A clever sea animal with a long nose
B. Do
C. An exciting ride
D. An exciting place to visit
E. Clever acts

Down

1. A huge sea animal
2. Things to buy
3. Opposite of "same"
4. A body of water like an ocean

15

Marineland Scavenger Hunt

C. Read each clue and spell the word.

1. I come out at night and provide light.
   ___ ___ ___

2. I'm red and round, and I'm a fruit.
   ___ ___ ___ ___ ___

3. I'm the colour of an apple.
   ___ ___ ___

4. I'm a letter that sounds the same as "eye".
   ___

5. Birds live in me.
   ___ ___ ___ ___

6. I'm the opposite of "difficult".
   ___ ___ ___ ___

7. I'm a red bug with black spots.
   ___ ___ ___ ___ ___ ___ ___

8. I'm a little insect. I can't fly.
   ___ ___ ___

9. I'm the opposite of "day".
   ___ ___ ___ ___ ___

10. I'm a pet. I bark when I'm mad.
    ___ ___ ___

Now, write the circled letters in order.

___ ___ ___ ___ ___ ___ ___ ___ ___ ___
 1   2   3   4   5   6   7   8   9   10

D. The following pictures are about Marineland. Write a sentence about each.

Challenge

Draw a picture of yourself doing fun things at Marineland and write a sentence to describe it.

PROGRESS TEST 2

A. Underline the noun in each of the following phrases.

1. the cute <u>doll</u>
2. four new <u>books</u>
3. a new <u>bike</u>
4. a little <u>cat</u>
5. a spotted <u>dog</u>
6. six melting <u>popsicles</u>
7. the soft <u>pillow</u>
8. the brick <u>house</u>
9. a funny <u>clown</u>
10. the green <u>plant</u>
11. a tidy <u>bed</u>
12. my first <u>car</u>
13. an empty <u>glass</u>
14. the bright <u>light</u>
15. a tall <u>tree</u>
16. his baseball <u>cap</u>
17. a pretty <u>girl</u>
18. a brave <u>firefighter</u>
19. a crowded <u>street</u>
20. a wooden <u>box</u>
21. a sunny <u>day</u>
22. a big <u>breakfast</u>
23. a winding <u>road</u>
24. a huge <u>whale</u>

B. Read the clues. Complete the crossword puzzle with the words that mean the opposite.

Across
A. small
B. full
C. hard
D. short
E. thin

Down
1. hate
2. no
3. slow
4. heavy
5. bright

PROGRESS TEST 2

C. Unscramble the sentences and write them on the lines.

Remember to begin each sentence with a capital letter and end it with a period.

1. favourite   are   my   candies   jujubes

   _____

2. is   Judy   good   friend   my   sister's

   _____

3. good   summer   ice cream   in   is   so

   _____

4. people   Toronto   visit   many   Zoo

   _____

5. swimming   I   go   like   to

   _____

6. read   of   we   lot   books   a

   _____

7. work   many   for   hours   firefighters

   _____

8. dolphins   sea   clever   animals   are

   _____

D. Read each of the following sentences. Circle the word in ( ) that means the same as the one in the shaded box.

1. The big dog jumped up on me.
   (large   tall)

 2. There was a tiny kitten at the pet store.
   (tidy   small)

3. Mom walked very fast towards me.
   (quickly   carefully)

 4. We have been to Marineland once.
   (one time   every time)

5. The clever boy answered all the questions.
   (smart   cute)

6. Look at my beautiful dress.
   (new   pretty)

7. My dad has a lot of work to do.
   (much   more)

 8. Our neighbour is a nice old lady.
   (kind   rich)

E. Write a rhyming word for each of the following words.

1. rest
2. cup
3. sick
4. read
5. few
6. say
7. treat
8. real
9. four
10. rain
11. tale
12. burn
13. ate
14. land
15. stop
16. ever
17. care
18. neat
19. fill
20. paid
21. bug
22. give
23. pull
24. told

F. Each of the following sentences has a misspelled word. Circle the misspelled word and write the correct spelling in the box.

1. The trane arrives late.
2. Many peeple like to eat ice cream.
3. Jo and her fiends are playing in the park.
4. The bluejays are eating seads in the garden.
5. There are many advanture parks in Canada.
6. The plum is a juicy friut.
7. The children are petting the whale.
8. We had a picnic lunch on the glass.
9. Penquins are cute animals.
10. We play soccer in the big feeld.

1.	2.
3.	4.
5.	6.
7.	8.
9.	10.

1

Join each frog to a lily pad to form a word.

2. Percy the Piglet wants to save his pocket money into a piggy bank. Colour the coins with "money" words to make a path to the piggy bank.

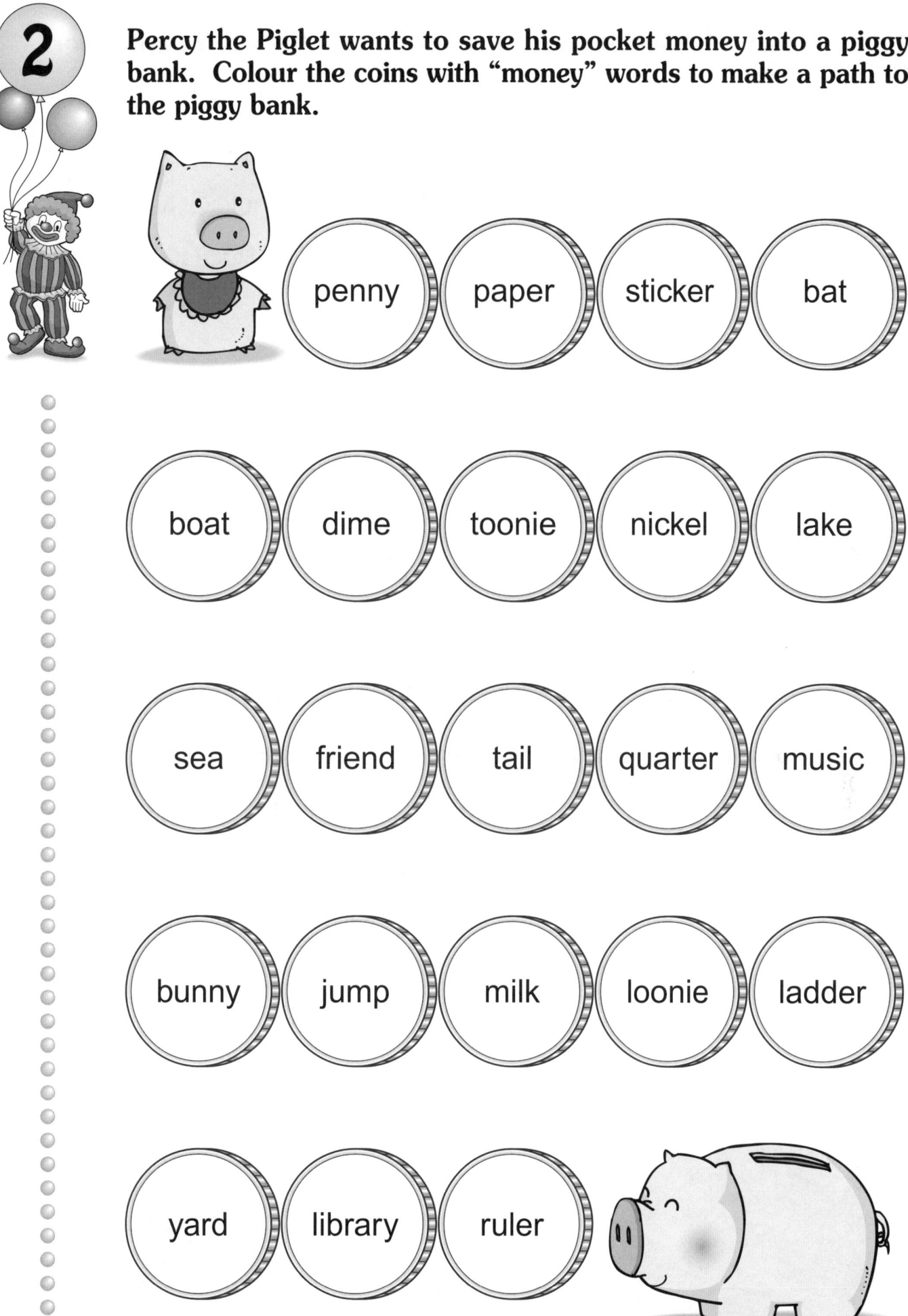

3 Nellie is having fun on the beach. Circle the words in the word search.

sunglasses   sand   umbrella
swimsuit   pail   sandcastle
lifebelt   seagull   spade
hat   towel   shell   sun

s	b	l	i	f	e	b	e	l	t
u	a	q	c	k	v	s	o	p	o
n	m	n	s	g	d	u	e	a	w
g	p	b	d	o	j	n	w	i	e
l	m	h	r	c	s	h	e	l	l
a	k	c	t	e	a	w	a	z	s
s	a	n	d	o	l	s	j	t	p
s	e	a	g	u	l	l	t	y	a
e	x	r	l	e	n	v	a	l	d
s	w	i	m	s	u	i	t	e	e

4 Circle the word that does not belong in each balloon.

1. drum, guitar, flute, radio, piano

2. camel, horse, elephant, squirrel, dolphin

3. muffin, cake, fish, bread, cookie

4. fin, pin, pen, tin, win

5. ten, seven, second, five, eight

5

Find one word hidden in each of the words. Write it in the ◯.

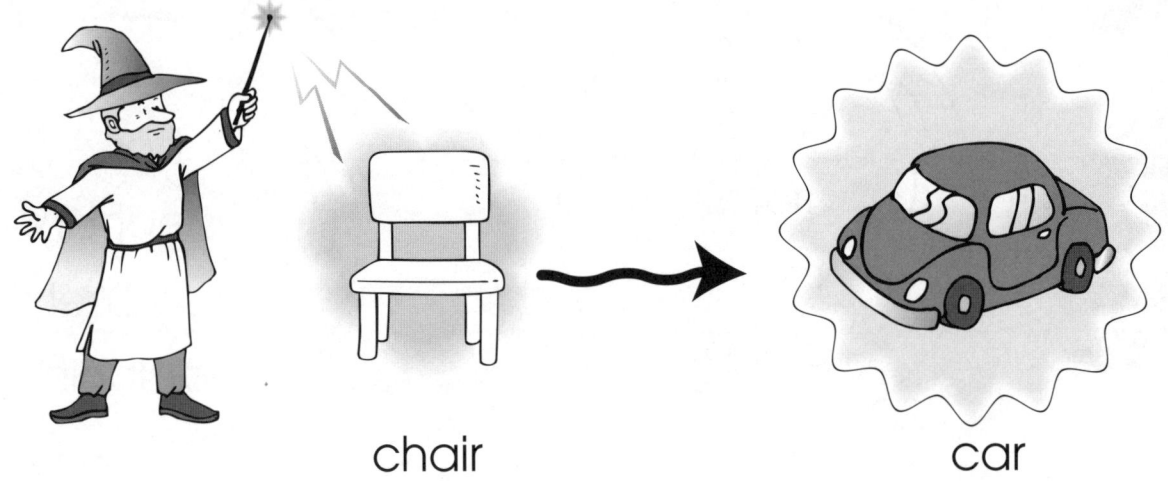

chair → car

1. second →
2. flavour →
3. paper →
4. baked →
5. special →
6. house →

6 Count and colour the fish Uncle Fred has caught by following the letters in the words "A great catch". Write the number on the pail.

7

Read the clues and complete the crossword puzzle.

Across

1. This pet likes to run on a turning wheel.
4. A canary is one.
6. This pet may be named Porky.
7. If your pet rabbit was named King Rabbitoh, what would its initials be?
9. Another name for a rabbit
12. Birds need these to fly to their perch.
13. A bird's claws are its ___ .

Down

1. What pet cats like to drink
2. A pet frog or a pet snake may lay these.
3. We keep these in a bowl or tank.
5. This pet has been called "Man's Best Friend".
8. Bugs Bunny is one.
10. Rabbits like to twitch their ___ .
11. Pet birds are kept in a ___ .

8 Look at the cute baby animals. Write what they are.

piglet   cub   puppy
duckling   fawn   calf

1. I'm a _____ .

2. I'm a _____ .

3. I'm a _____ .

4. I'm a _____ .

5. I'm a _____ .

6. I'm a _____ .

9 Put the puzzle pieces in the correct places. Write the letters on the blank pieces. What does each picture show?

10 Help Liz the Lizard find her way up the wall by colouring the two-syllable words.

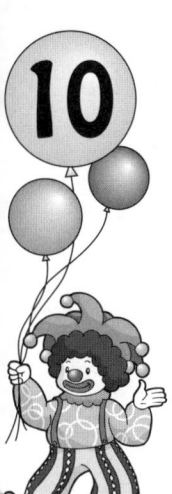

reporter	block	kitten	easier
old	today	furry
together	under	toast	hen
through	behind	winter
sail	cheap	ring	pocket
family	sister	balloon

11 Match the clouds with words that rhyme. Colour each pair the same colour.

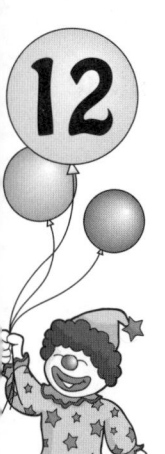

12

Sandra and her classmates are visiting the farm. Circle the animals in the word search.

duck　　sheep　　horse　　goat
pig　　goose　　turkey　　rabbit
cow　　chicken　　pigeon　　dog

c	m	g	o	s	p	r	a	c	x	a	p
g	h	o	r	s	e	a	f	o	t	c	i
k	d	t	a	h	o	d	u	p	e	l	e
n	y	x	b	k	c	o	w	i	t	o	s
s	a	u	b	c	t	g	o	g	a	q	h
o	e	d	i	g	o	o	s	e	b	a	e
d	t	u	t	p	a	r	a	o	b	t	e
v	m	c	h	i	c	k	e	n	i	b	p
g	c	k	d	g	d	s	m	h	f	w	r
o	r	c	n	v	p	z	e	z	q	x	n
a	j	u	o	a	x	g	b	y	u	d	w
t	u	r	k	e	y	c	s	b	v	t	k

13 Help Monica open the treasure chest by entering the code. Follow the letters in the words "treasure hunt" to get the code.

14

Help the zookeeper write the names of the animals.

1.

2.

3.

4.

5.

6.

15

Read the clues and complete the crossword puzzle.

Across

1. A worker bee has this many stings.
3. These are also stinging insects.
6. This insect can be annoying and it may carry diseases.
8. These jumping insects make a shrill chirping sound.
9. An insect with hard feelers (some are tiny but others are quite large)
11. These insects can spoil your picnic!

Down

2. Where wasps and other insects lay their eggs
4. These tiny insects can carry heavy loads.
5. A queen bee does this to other queens.
6. This insect of the night is attracted by light.
7. Some people think most insects are ____ .
8. People walk but creepy crawlies ____ .
9. Its home is a hive.
10. An insect hatches from this.

16 Help Mother Hen find her eggs by colouring the eggs that ryhme with "hen".

17

Little Carol wants to make an animal-sticker album. Help her colour the stickers with "animal" words.

- walrus
- penguin
- tiger
- cheetah
- sock
- belt
- sweater
- skunk
- fox
- beaver
- jumper
- boots
- tie
- ostrich
- skirt
- vest
- wolf
- rabbit
- blouse
- whale
- bow
- coat

18 Find ten "colour" words in the word search. Colour the picture with all the ten colours.

c	p	k	g	s	f	r	e	l	a	p	h
f	i	q	x	m	o	w	h	i	t	e	n
h	n	b	p	c	u	b	l	y	v	k	i
d	k	a	o	w	g	r	e	e	n	o	t
b	g	t	r	n	c	o	j	l	w	x	f
l	m	e	a	y	m	w	b	l	u	e	r
a	i	p	n	d	g	n	h	o	a	s	d
c	n	u	g	r	q	i	t	w	l	z	j
k	s	r	e	d	k	z	c	o	q	b	v
o	j	a	v	e	p	u	r	p	l	e	m

Complete EnglishSmart • Grade 2

Look at the code and the pictures. Write what Lilian says.

1	2	3	4	5	6	7	8	9	10	11	12	13
A	B	C	D	E	F	G	H	I	J	K	L	M

14	15	16	17	18	19	20	21	22	23	24	25	26
N	O	P	Q	R	S	T	U	V	W	X	Y	Z

13, 25   14, 1, 21, 7, 8, 20, 25

8, 9, 4, 5, 19   8, 9, 19   6, 1, 22, 15, 21, 18, 9, 20, 5

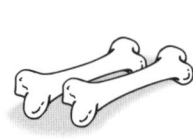 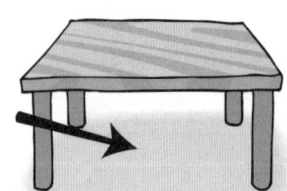   13, 25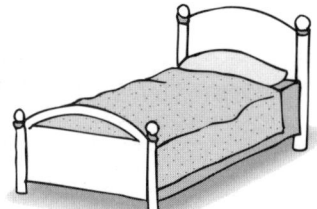

_____

_____

_____

_____

20

Read the clues and complete the crossword puzzle.

Across

1. This very large fruit is green on the outside and red and watery on the inside; it has black seeds.
4. A very juicy yellow fruit shaped a bit like a heart
6. Fruits are nice to ___ .
7. Before eating an orange, you must ___ it.
9. A yellow fruit with a stone inside
10. Strawberries are this colour.

Down

2. This fruit can be green, red, or yellow; it has a core.
3. The name of this fruit is the same as its colour.
5. You should only eat fruits if they are ___ ; otherwise you might get a stomach ache.
7. This soft pink fruit is fleshy and has a large stone inside.
8. Taste of a lemon.

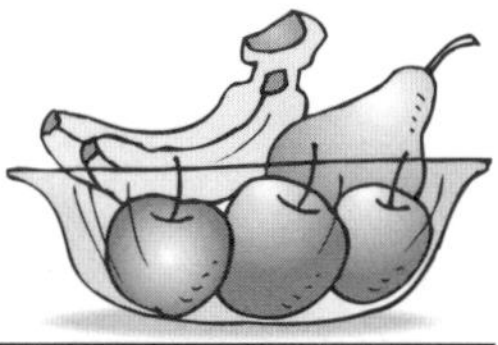

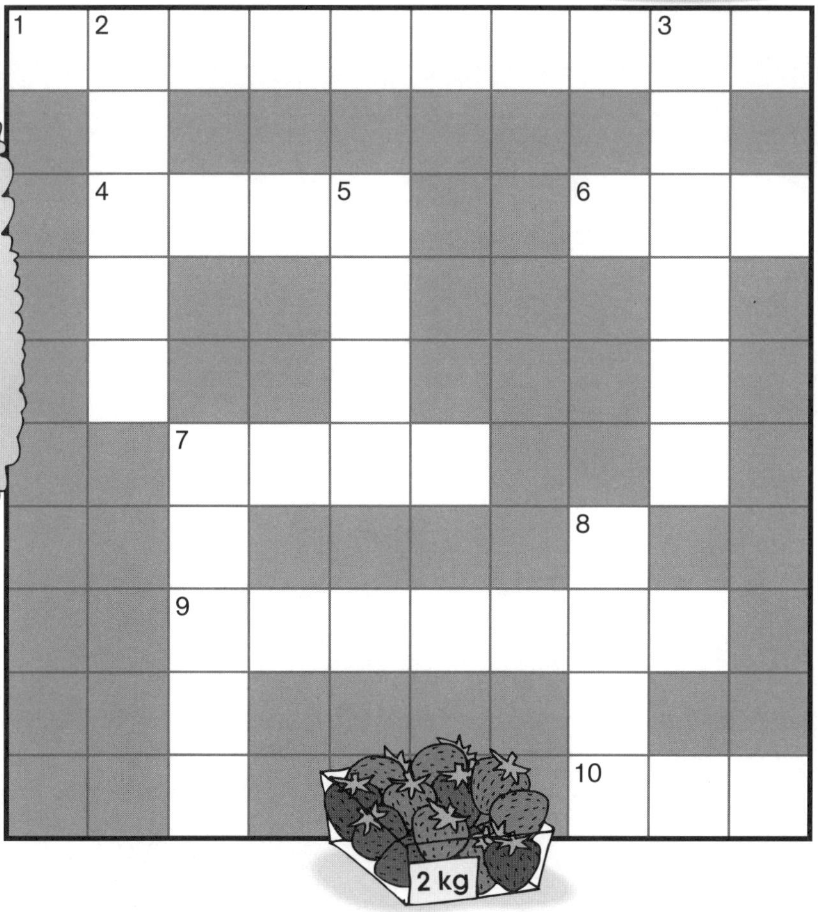

Section 1 Answers — Grade 2

1 The Bumblebee

A.
1. An insect.
2. It is yellow and black and has six legs.
3. The queen bee.
4. In the nest.
5. After a winter in hibernation.
6. They make honey from the nectar in flowering plants.

B.
1. leaf   2. pail
3. cap   4. bat
5. mop   6. jug
7. yarn   8. goat
9. wagon 10. rabbit
11. drum 12. top
13. fan   14. web
15. sun   16. queen
17. hat

C.
1. Polar bears live in the Arctic. They are big and white. They have <u>big paws</u>. They have small eyes and ears. They <u>jump from ice floe to ice floe</u>.
2. Polar bears have other names. They are <u>sometimes called white bears, sea bears, or ice bears</u>. The polar bears <u>swim very well</u>.
3. Polar bears move fast and travel far. They <u>eat seals and fish</u>. The male is usually larger than the female. They have <u>hairy feet</u>.
4. Baby bears or cubs are born in winter. They <u>weigh 2 pounds when born</u>. They <u>remain with their mothers from 10 months to 2 years</u>.

D.
1. A square is a shape with four equal sides.
2. A triangle is a shape with three sides.
3. A circle is a single line.
4. A rectangle is a shape with opposite sides that are equal.

2 The Museum Trip

A. 1. B 2. B 3. B 4. C

B.
1. bus   2. box
3. nest   4. dime
5. tulip   6. seven
7. mask   8. bar
9. pot   10. pen
11. lemon   12. acorn
13. can   14. beehive
15. bone   16. ball
17. sunflower 18. sock
19. saw   20. log
21. kite   22. rope
23. rake

C.
1. We start school in the autumn.
2. My school is close to home.
3. I walk to and from school every day.
4. Sometimes, I go home for lunch.
5. There are lots of sports at my school.
6. We play soccer, hockey, and volleyball.
7. I like to play floor games.

D.
1. ✔ Hockey
2. ✔ Hockey ; Football
3. ✔ Football
4. ✔ Hockey ; Football
5. ✔ Football
6. ✔ Hockey
7. ✔ Hockey ; Football
8. ✔ Hockey ; Football

3 The Eurotunnel

A.
1. In 1993.
2. The English Channel.
3. Two are for trains to carry people and one is for service.
4. Rob.

B.
1. lamp   2. web   3. mop   4. jug
5. pot   6. bag   7. desk   8. bell
9. net   10. can   11. lips 12. fan
13. tent 14. rock 15. six   16. nut

C.
1. Apples   2. The CN Tower
3. A hexagon   4. The time
5. A computer   6. Skating
7. The Earth   8. (Answer will vary.)

D.
1. cup ; bowl ; glass
2. Triceratops ; Tyrannosaurus ; Stegosaurus
3. blackboard ; desk ; eraser
4. tires ; horn ; key
5. swing ; seesaw ; slide
6. pear ; grapes ; apple

4 Snakes

A.
1. reptiles   2. long
3. cold   4. eggs
5. laid   6. hibernation
7. skins   8. move
9. place

B.
1. bike   2. cube   3. hive   4. pole
5. cake   6. cone   7. five   8. kite
9. cane   10. tube 11. tulip 12. rope
13. hole 14. gate 15. ruler 16. lake

C. (Answers will vary.)

D. 1. recipe   2. box

Section 1 Answers

3. ingredients
4. cupboard
5. refrigerator
6. pot ; stove ; melted
7. square

5 What Happens Next?

A. (Answers will vary.)
B.
1. snail
2. day
3. nail
4. jay
5. tray
6. paint
7. tail
8. pay
9. say
10. play

C. (Order may vary.)
1. The monkey likes to hang by its tail.
2. At the zoo, we visit the animals.
3. The African elephant is the largest living land animal.
4. The zebra is black and white.
5. The male lion has a mane on its neck.
6. The tiger is orange and black.
7. The zookeeper helps clean the cages.

D. (word search grid)

6 Days of the Week

A. (Suggested answers)
1. Easter Sunday.
2. he will go to the beach.
3. he will ride on the roller coaster.
4. he will go to the library.
5. he will paint a picture.
6. he will go to the playground.
7. (Answer will vary.)

B.
1. bee
2. jeans
3. tea
4. team
5. bean
6. meat
7. weed
8. week
9. sea
10. seed
11. beak

C. (Answers will vary.)
D.
1. Sunday ; Monday ; Tuesday ; Wednesday ; Thursday ; Friday ; Saturday
2. January ; February ; March ; April ; May ; June ; July ; August ; September ; October ; November ; December

7 The CN Tower

A.
1. self-supporting tower in the world.
2. five and one-half football fields.
3. as deep as a five-storey building.
4. improve the broadcasting of radio and television signals.
5. a person hopping down its 1,967 steps on a pogo stick.

B.
1. flowers
2. clowns
3. slide
4. sleep
5. glass
6. sled
7. flag
8. blew
9. plate
10. glad
11. clock
12. play

C. (Answers will vary.)
D. (Suggested answers)

1.
2.
3.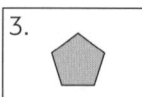
4.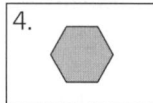
5.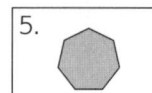
6.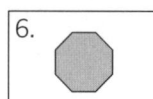

8 Sir John A. Macdonald

A.
1. Sir John A. Macdonald.
2. In Glasgow, Scotland.
3. Five.
4. 1867.
5. Completing the Pacific Railway.
6. In Ottawa.

B. (Suggested answers)
1. prune
2. prime
3. crop
4. grip
5. grape
6. bring
7. cream
8. fruit
9. braid
10. grass
11. brass
12. prize
13. tree
14. free
15. frog
16. drum
17. dress
18. truck
19. crab
20. breed

Grade 2

21. greed		22. creed		
23. freed		24. frame		
25. green		26. drone		
27. crime		28. grime		
29. trap		30. trail		
31. true		32. broom		

C. (Answers will vary.)
D. 1. the fourth 2. the tenth
   3. the second 4. the fifth
   5. the third   6. the seventh
   7. the ninth   8. the first
   9. the sixth   10. the eighth

Progress Test 1

A. 1. road ; toad ; load
   2. like ; bike ; hike ; pike
   3. game ; came ; tame ; name
   4. bake ; take ; cake ; lake ; rake
   5. day ; jay ; ray ; say ; way ; May

B. 1. vase   2. drum
   3. jug   4. pin
   5. nest   6. gate
   7. mop   8. leaf
   9. fan   10. yarn
   11. hat   12. sock
   13. web   14. six
   15. cap

C. 1. tube   2. cake
   3. log   4. bone
   5. pole   6. hive
   7. tent   8. fish
   9. cube   10. rake
   11. five   12. hand

D. (word search grid)

E. 1. Kathleen loves chocolate cake. ; T
   2. Will David take out the garbage? ; A
   3. They shop at the mall. ; T
   4. I won the first prize! ; E
   5. Do you like ice cream? ; A
   6. Oh no! ; E

F. 1. car ; (drove) ; highway
   2. bird ; (laid) ; eggs ; nest
   3. Mom ; (bakes) ; cakes ; home
   4. Tom ; (walks) ; school ; day
   5. She ; (likes) ; (take) ; dog ; walk

G. (Answers will vary.)

H. 2. C   3. E   4. F   5. H
   6. I   7. J   8. A   9. D
   10. G

9 Dance Lessons

A. 1. three   2. ballet
   3. slippers   4. day
   5. ten   6. ballet
   7. many   8. good
   9. eighteen   10. dance
   11. dances   12. costumes
   13. fun   14. jive
   15. A   16. B

B. 1. smells   2. space
   3. stairs   4. stove
   5. snake   6. skunk
   7. snack   8. swim
   9. skip   10. small
   11. swat   12. snip
   13. snap   14. spoon

C. 1. Fetch the bone, Punkie.
   2. Punkie, go and get the newspaper.
   3. Find the shoe, Punkie.
   4. Take the leash in your mouth.
   5. Find the toy.
   6. Don't chase the car.

D. 1. penny   2. toonie
   3. dime   4. quarter
   5. loonie   6. nickel

10 The Treasure Chest

A. (Suggested answers)
   1. Hearing about a sunken ship in the Shallow Sea.
   2. Searching for the sunken treasure.
   3. Finding the sunken treasure.

B. 1. She sells sea shells by the sea shore.
   2. Chester chewed the chewing gum cheerily.
   3. Thaddeus thought the thimble was thick.
   4. Willy the whale whirled while the wheel of the white whaler whistled.

C. 1. whiskers   2. thick
   3. ship   4. chest
   5. peach   6. moth

Section 1 Answers

D. 1. F 2. E 3. K 4. A
5. C 6. J 7. M 8. B
9. D 10. L 11. H 12. G
13. I 14. S 15. W 16. U
17. Y 18. X 19. V 20. N
21. P 22. R 23. Z 24. O
25. Q 26. T

E. 1. horse 2. cow
3. rabbit 4. dog
5. kangaroo 6. pig
7. chicken 8. goose
9. cat 10. deer

11 A Visit to the Farm

A. There are <u>many</u> different kinds of <u>farms</u>. Some are <u>dairy</u> farms and some are <u>cattle</u> farms. There are others that grow <u>vegetables</u>, like <u>corn</u>, <u>potatoes</u>, and <u>carrots</u>. In the West, farmers grow <u>wheat</u>.

We <u>visited</u> a farm with our <u>class</u>. It was a <u>dairy</u> farm, so the animals were all <u>cows</u>. The farmer <u>showed</u> us how the cows are <u>milked</u> using big machines.

We had lots of <u>fun</u> at the <u>farm</u>.
1. Different kinds of farms.
2. A dairy farm.

B. Arnie's <u>farm</u> is <u>far</u> from the <u>market</u>. Every day, Arnie <u>works</u> very <u>hard</u>. He <u>turns</u> the soil, which is sometimes called <u>dirt</u>. When there are lots of <u>worms</u> in the soil, it is healthy. There are also lots of animals on the <u>farm</u>. Some are <u>horses</u> and others are pigs, from which Arnie gets <u>pork</u> to sell at the market.

C. 1. Mark 2. Ottawa
3. Venus 4. Mrs. Smith
5. Sun 6. Punkie
7. Portland Drive 8. Mars
9. Canada Day 10. Sunday
11. Deer Lake 12. The Gap
13. Charlotte's Web 14. May
15. Humber 16. Air Canada
17. Park Street School

D. 1. English 2. Spanish
3. France 4. Hungarian
5. Romanian 6. Italian
7. Greek

E. 1. ITALIAN 2. SPANISH
3. HUNGARIAN

12 Out on the Town

A. 1. A 2. D 3. F 4. E
5. C 6. B

B. cl<u>ow</u>n : town ; brown ; flowers ; crown
h<u>ou</u>se : hound ; blouse ; couch ; mouse ; sound
sn<u>ow</u>man : grow ; blow ; row ; glow ; rainbow ; low

C. 2. 4 cars 3. 10 flowers
4. 2 boys 5. 5 bicycles
6. 7 trees 7. 9 parking meters
8. 3 trucks

D. 1. E 2. D 3. B 4. A
5. C

13 My Cookbook Recipe – Blueberry Muffins

A. 1. muffins 2. wet
3. blueberries 4. egg
5. 400°F

B. 1. cook 2. book
3. look 4. cookbook
5. fool 6. pool
7. cool 8. drool

C. (Answers will vary.)

D. 1. crying 2. breezy
3. tired 4. little
5. damp 6. big
7. hard 8. dirty

14 The Coin Collection

A. 1. coin collection.
2. three hundred coins.
3. three coins from Italy.
4. him gifts of coins.
5. all over the world.
6. coin is one from Sri Lanka.
7. large and heavy.
8. a hole in the centre.

B. 1. coin 2. boy
3. joy 4. point
5. soy 6. annoy
7. boil 8. toy
9. Oil 10. loyal

C. 1. are 2. am
3. is 4. is
5. are 6. are
7. are 8. am
9. is 10. is

D. 1. cold 2. short
3. thin 4. wet
5. sad 6. healthy
7. white 8. brave
9. answer

15 Autumn

A.
1. season 2. Summer
3. fall 4. beautiful
5. because 6. colour
7. ground 8. carpet
9. hike 10. animals
11. woods 12. fawn
13. woods

B.
1. Autumn.
2. They change colour and fall to the ground.
3. In the woods.
4. Fall.
5. Winter.

C.
1. fawn 2. straw
3. Autumn 4. saw
5. yawn 6. saucer
7. auto 8. jaw

D.
1. are 2. build
3. has 4. like
5. live 6. consists
7. breed 8. warn

E.
1. S 2. H 3. A 4. A
5. S 6. A 7. A 8. A
9. H

16 All about Plants

A. Most <u>plants</u> start as a <u>seed</u>. Usually, you <u>plant</u> the <u>seed</u> in the <u>garden</u> of the <u>yard</u>, in <u>shade</u> or <u>sun</u>.

If you use a small <u>trowel</u>, you can dig a <u>hole</u> just big enough to <u>poke</u> the seed down and <u>cover</u> it with more <u>soil</u>.

First, you <u>plant</u> the <u>seed</u> and let the <u>sun</u> shine down on it. After a few <u>weeks</u>, little shoots begin to <u>sprout</u>. Then, the <u>stem</u> gets stronger and <u>leaves</u> begin to show.

B.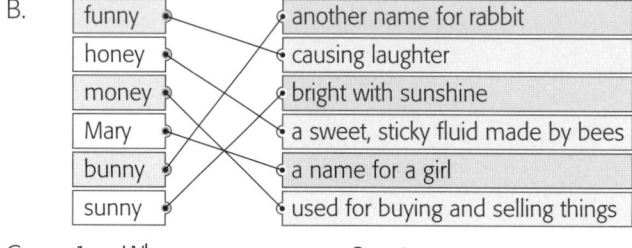

C.
1. Why 2. try
3. fly 4. shy
5. my

D.

(crossword)
Across: A. planted, B. wanted, C. trained, D. learned, E. asked
Down: 1. treasured, 2. smiled, 3. plays, 4. answered, 5. helped, 6. weeded

E.
1. December 2. September
3. February 4. October
5. January 6. June
7. August 8. November
9. March 10. April
11. May 12. July

17 Penguins

A.
1. Antarctica ; Africa ; Australia
2. Blue Fairy
3. 40 cm
4. Emperor ; 120 cm
5. fish ; squid ; small shrimp
6. Leopard seals ; killer whales
7. female (penguin) ; male (penguin)

B.
1. grow ; gate ; goose ; girl ; goat ; game
2. giant ; gem ; giraffe ; gym
3. cake ; clown ; cook ; crate ; count
4. cent ; cell ; city

C.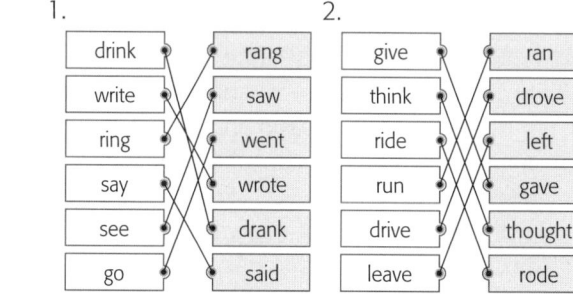

Section 1 Answers — Grade 2

3.
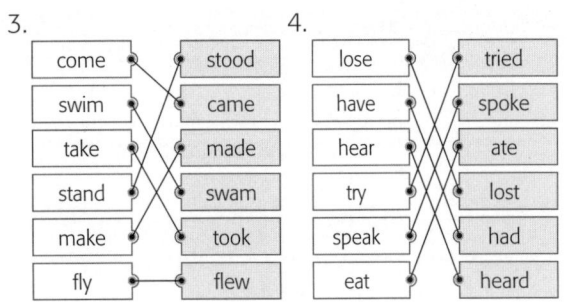

come — stood
swim — came
take — made
stand — swam
make — took
fly — flew

4.
lose — tried
have — spoke
hear — ate
try — lost
speak — had
eat — heard

D. Word search with: monitor, diskettes, printer, modem, disc, cds

Progress Test 2

A.
1. oceans
2. while
3. small
4. plates
5. chew
6. whole
7. length
8. weigh
9. smell
10. pitches
11. hold
12. breathing

B. David and his (friend), Chris, are going to visit the Hockey Hall of Fame in downtown Toronto, Canada. It is in a large (building) not far from Union Station, where the (friends) are taking the (subway) from Mississauga to Toronto.

There are so many exciting (exhibits) at the Hockey Hall of Fame. There are (pieces) of (equipment) worn by famous hockey (players), like Wayne Gretzky. The Stanley Cup, which is awarded to the top hockey (team) each (year), is sometimes on (display) there.

The (boys) want to see the first (mask) that was worn by Jacques Plante and some of the old hockey (uniforms) from (years) gone by. Maybe, if they're lucky, they might see a visiting hockey (player).

The last (thing) David and Chris go to see is all the (statistics) of (players) who broke many (records) over the (years). (Players) like Gordie Howe, Jean Beliveau, and Wayne Gretzky changed the (game) of (hockey) forever.

C. Canada is one of the largest countries in the world. It is one of three countries that make up North America. It is made up of ten provinces and three territories. Nunavut became the newest territory in 1999.

There are four Atlantic provinces and three of them are called Maritime provinces.

There are also three Prairie provinces.

D.
1. went
2. is travelling
3. is
4. likes
5. fixes
6. plays
7. studies
8. skis
9. will go
10. tries
11. takes
12. go
13. bake
14. laughs
15. watch

E.
1. large
2. cry
3. tiny
4. run
5. sad
6. hop

F.
1. sale
2. sea
3. pear
4. mail
5. blue
6. vane

G.
1. bright
2. dry
3. clean
4. close
5. happy
6. heavy

H.
1. e   2. i   3. e   4. i
5. i   6. i   7. e   8. e
9. i   10. e   11. e   12. e
13. e   14. i   15. e   16. i
17. i   18. e

Section 2 Answers — Grade 2

1 Nouns (1)

A. swing – ring ; fox – box ; block – lock ; beet – feet ; frog – log ; hat – bat ; bee – key ; fish – dish
B. (Suggested answers)
   1. bat ; hat ; mat ; rat ; vat
   2. car ; jar ; star
   3. jig ; pig ; wig
C. Nouns – cup ; candle ; balloon ; glove ; smile ; lamp ; hat ; flower
D. 1. pear   2. man
   3. table   4. dog
   5. moon   6. pot
   7. jacket   8. fence
   9. pencil   10. sky
  11. ocean   12. door
  13. truck   14. finger
E. (Any order)
   Person: boy ; girl ; mother ; doctor ; man ; baby ; woman ; Mr. Smith ; postman ; Maria
   Place: city ; Alberta ; school ; Ottawa ; Ontario ; Wonderland ; park ; Toronto ; village ; town
   Thing: penguin ; orange ; balloon ; banana ; lamp ; bike ; sun ; candle ; radio ; television ; glass ; finger ; ring

2 Nouns (2)

A. (Answers will vary.)
B. (Any order)
   Yukon ; Toronto ; Victoria ; Regina ; St. John's ; Halifax ; Montreal ; Canada ; Edmonton ; Winnipeg ; Vancouver ; Calgary ; Quebec City ; Fredericton ; Ottawa
C. 1. star ; sky   2. leaves ; tree
   3. cat ; fur   4. days ; week
   5. clock   6. lunch
   7. bus ; mall   8. car
   9. dog ; rug   10. photos
D. 3. C   4. P   5. C
   6. C   7. C   8. P
   9. C   10. P   11. C
  12. P   13. C   14. P
E. 1. School ; September
   2. Andrew ; car ; Pepe
   3. CN Tower ; building ; Canada
   4. bike ; path ; Loblaws
   5. Anne ; Bob ; dog ; park
   6. Tuesday ; day ; week

3 Plural Nouns

A. Singular nouns:
   cat ; cup ; pan ; finger ; gate ; chair ; can ; cake ; bag ; bug ; grape ; bottle
   Plural nouns:
   bees ; dogs ; apples ; pots ; faces ; trees ; tables ; cookies
B. boxes ; trees ; axes ; kisses ; hands ; yards ; books ; cakes ; bikes ; flowers ; bags ; passes ; taxes ; buses ; cars ; mixes ; glasses ; foxes ; gases ; parks ; cookies ; dreams ; mittens ; eggs ; beds ; coats ; shops
C. One: brush ; patch ; bench
   More than one: wishes ; lunches
D. 1. peaches   2. kisses
   3. wishes   4. churches
   5. fishes
E. 1. chair   2. book
   3. car   4. bus
   5. McDonald's   6. refrigerator
   7. bike   8. fingers
   9. snow   10. orange
  11. eyes   12. sun

4 Pronouns

A. 1. I   2. me
   3. We   4. us
   5. me   6. I
   7. me   8. We
   9. us
B. (Answers will vary.)
C. 1. She   2. her
   3. She   4. her
   5. she   6. her
   7. He   8. her
   9. he   10. He
  11. her
D. 1. they   2. it
   3. they   4. it
   5. it   6. they
   7. them   8. They
   9. them   10. they
  11. they
E. 1. They ; them   2. She
   3. It ; it   4. It
   5. they   6. her
   7. his   8. them
   9. You   10. he

Section 2 Answers

5 Verbs (1)

A. 1. skates 2. walk
   3. drinks 4. bakes
   5. draw 6. runs
   7. sings 8. play
   9. throws

B. Can See:
   go ; eat ; run ; see ; get ; talk ; sleep ; make ; drive ;
   cook ; look ; play ; work ; touch ; walk ; ask ; do ; write ;
   watch ; throw ; move
   Cannot See:
   start ; try ; learn ; listen ; hear ; think ; feel

C. 1. swinging 2. growing
   3. blowing 4. skating
   5. climbing 6. falling

D. 1. shines 2. burn
   3. likes 4. eat
   5. rocks

E. 1. walks – S 2. talked – S
   3. listens – C 4. feels – C
   5. learns – C 6. cooks – S
   7. drives – S 8. looked – S
   9. see – S 10. think – C ; can do – S

6 Verbs (2)

A. 1. painted 2. pulled
   3. wished 4. kicked
   5. played 6. sewed
   A. talked B. walked
   C. crawled

B. say – said ; ring – rang ; drive – drove ; lose – lost ;
   swim – swam
   drink – drank ; stand – stood ; run – ran ; take – took ;
   make – made

C. 1. had 2. saw 3. left
   4. wrote 5. stood 6. flew

D. 1. is 2. am 3. is
   4. are 5. am 6. is
   7. are 8. are 9. is
   10. is 11. are

E. 1. is 2. are 3. are
   4. is 5. are 6. are
   7. is 8. are 9. are
   10. is 11. are 12. are

7 Verbs (3)

A. 1. was 2. was 3. were
   4. was

B. 1. was 2. were 3. was
   4. was 5. were

C. 1. Helping Verb – has ; Main Verb – talked
   2. Helping Verb – has ; Main Verb – visited
   3. Helping Verb – are ; Main Verb – hiking
   4. Helping Verb – did ; Main Verb – give
   5. Helping Verb – is ; Main Verb – walking
   6. Helping Verb – had ; Main Verb – worked

D. 1. are 2. are
   3. has 4. has
   5. is 6. is
   7. feed 8. is
   9. is 10. is
   11. is 12. likes

E. 1. is 2. bought
   3. took 4. flew
   5. wind 6. was ; were
   7. is flying 8. opened
   9. brought 10. wound
   11. packed ; left

Progress Test 1

A. top ; bed ; bird ; hat ; ball ; web ; log ; leaf ; pear ; pan ;
   jug ; goat ; apple

B. 1. ring 2. cup
   3. log 4. milk
   5. sun 6. pan

C. (Suggested answers)
   1. bat ; hat ; mat ; rat
   2. bog ; fog ; jog ; log
   3. bug ; hug ; mug ; rug

D. 1. Marie ; James ; bikes ; park
   2. Mr. Long ; game ; SkyDome ; Tuesday
   3. magician ; wand ; audience ; cloud ; smoke
   4. Rudy ; hedgehog ; garage ; chips
   5. Andrew ; bus ; Main Street
   6. boat ; Lake Ontario
   7. movie ; *Peter Pan*
   8. dogs ; Credit Valley Pet Hospital
   9. mom ; Toronto
   10. day ; Wonderland

E. 1. He 2. She 3. It
   4. They 5. He 6. it

F.
a	p	a	r	w	u	a	s	h	v	f	t	r	h	e
n	r	c	e	a	r	r	i	d	e	l	h	s	j	i
c	l	i	m	b	a	t	u	s	n	y	s	f	e	k
l	e	l	i	l	d	m	c	o	c	w	v	c	t	l
o	u	d	s	q	l	s	v	b	h	b	x	s	d	t
k	s	h	w	r	r	u	n	r	s	h	t	a	l	k
s	v	v	i	o	f	g	k	i	c	k	h	m	a	f
u	f	s	m	t	g	u	s	v	u	t	i	h	e	f
v	s	r	f	s	d	r	i	n	k	e	n	s	p	s
h	m	a	l	k	n	t	s	p	s	v	k	c	j	y
u	e	t	h	a	o	b	e	l	k	o	m	e	u	a
r	l	h	i	k	t	c	p	l	a	y	b	f	m	d
s	l	i	d	e	s	d	l	h	t	r	l	t	p	s

G. 1. moved 2. touched
3. watch 4. worked
5. watch

H. 1. learned 2. Did ; try ; climb
3. cooks 4. can make
5. talks 6. makes

8 Adjectives

A. 1. thin 2. bright
3. dirty 4. rainy
5. high 6. hard

B. 1. strong 2. shiny
3. broken 4. orange

C. 1. short - size 2. square - shape
3. tiny - size 4. wide - size
5. tall - size 6. large - size
7. oval - shape 8. huge - size
9. round - shape 10. sharp - shape
11. long - size 12. high - size

D. 1. round 2. sharp
3. tiny 4. huge
5. short 6. tall

E.
e	n	h	m	h	b	l	c	k	s	r	a	r	y
m	f	q	e	g	c	k	b	o	r	a	n	g	e
t	r	j	a	r	e	d	h	l	u	h	v	h	l
b	b	l	u	e	r	m	u	r	l	m	d	l	l
d	q	r	t	e	h	b	l	a	c	k	e	k	o
e	s	t	v	n	j	d	s	r	t	t	a	i	w

F. (Answers will vary.)

G. 1. dusty 2. delicious
3. green 4. rough
5. juicy 6. sharp

7. sweet 8. salty ; French
9. loud 10. brown

H. (Answers will vary.)

9 Articles

A. 1. a 2. an 3. a
4. a 5. an 6. a
7. an 8. a 9. a
10. a 11. an 12. an

B. 1. an 2. a 3. a
4. an 5. a

C. 1. The ; a 2. an
3. an 4. The
5. An 6. a / the ; an
7. the ; a / the 8. a / the
9. a 10. the

D. (Answers will vary.)
E. (Answers will vary.)

F. 1. A 2. N 3. P
4. V 5. N 6. V
7. V 8. P 9. A
10. P

G. 1. an 2. the 3. the
4. an 5. the 6. the
7. a

10 Recognizing Sentences

A. 1. N 2. S 3. S
4. N 5. S 6. S
7. N 8. S 9. N
10. S 11. S 12. N

B. 1. F 2. J 3. L
4. K 5. C 6. H
7. I 8. D 9. E
10. B 11. A 12. G

C. 1. The bridge is over the river.
2. The ball is on the grass.
3. The boat is on the water.
4. The butterfly is on the flower.
5. The fox chases the rabbit.
6. The egg is on the plate.
7. The apple is in front of the pear.
8. The water is in the glass.

D. 1. The lion is big.
2. I have a bike.
3. The boys play baseball.
4. Pat has a cute rabbit.

Complete EnglishSmart • Grade 2   261

Section 2 Answers

5. Sam likes the blue shoes.
6. We have a swing in our backyard.

11 Sentence Types

A. 1. NS   2. S   3. S
   4. NS   5. S
B. 1. Rabbits live in burrows.
   2. Bears live in dens.
   3. A pig lives in a sty.
   4. Monkeys live in jungles.
   5. Cats live in houses.
   6. Horses live in barns.
C. 1. Q   2. NQ   3. NQ
   4. Q   5. Q
D. 1. C   2. D   3. E
   4. F   5. A   6. B
E. 1. E   2. NE   3. E
   4. NE 5. E
F. 1. !   2. .   3. .
   4. .   5. !   6. !
   7. .   8. ?   9. ?
   10. ! 11. ! 12. ?
   13. ! 14. .
G. 1. C   2. C   3. NC
   4. C   5. NC
H. 1. Be a good girl. / Be very careful!
   2. Take me to your leader!
   3. Try to eat your dinner.
   4. Be very careful! / Be a good girl.
   5. Bring your doll here.
   6. Girls, have some cake.
   7. Stop right there!

12 Sentences

A. 1. The tree   2. Most plants
   3. The sun   4. Rain
B. 1. Plants   2. Roots
   3. The stem   4. Leaves
   5. The fruit
C. 1. brushes his horse's hair
   2. like to be patted
   3. need to be trained
   4. talk to the horses
D. (Answers will vary.)
E. (Answers will vary.)
F. 1. Subject – Clare and James
      Predicate – like to play video games
   2. Subject – Marie
      Predicate – went to the movie
   3. Subject – Tom
      Predicate – bought an ice cream cone
   4. Subject – Colin
      Predicate – waited for the bus
   5. Subject – Jorge
      Predicate – likes to cook
   6. Subject – Melissa
      Predicate – will take her friends with her
   7. Subject – The sun
      Predicate – came out from behind the clouds
   8. Subject – We
      Predicate – go for a walk every day
   9. Subject – Bears
      Predicate – sleep in the winter
   10. Subject – Monopoly
       Predicate – is my favourite game
G. (Answers will vary.)
H. 1. is looking at the boy
   2. is feeding the elephant
   3. is big
   4. are lovely
   5. are very happy

13 Punctuation and Capitalization

A. 1. We read *Goldilocks and the Three Bears* at school.
   2. There are many boats on the sea.
   3. I read *The Berenstein Bears* at school today.
   4. Do you like *Peter Pan*?
B. (Answers will vary.)
C. (Answers will vary.)
D. 1. The apples are turning red
   2. The chocolate milkshake tastes good
   3. A kid is a baby goat / A baby goat is a kid
   4. Do you know what a baby rabbit is
   5. We ate lunch at the restaurant
   6. Wow, what a great movie
   7. I hope you come too
   8. Do you want some pie
   9. I can't wait
E. 1. !   2. ?   3. ?
   4. .   5. !   6. ?
   7. .   8. ?   9. !
   10. ? 11. . 12. .
F. 1. The balloon looks like a moon.
   2. Did you go to the store?
   3. Help me, please!
   4. I will not go there.

14 Sentence Type Review

A. 1. S ; .   2. E ; !   3. E ; !
   4. S ; .   5. E ; !
B. 1. C ; .   2. Q ; ?   3. Q ; ?
   4. C ; .   5. Q ; ?   6. Q ; ?
   7. C ; .
C. 1. Janet   2. The song
   3. We   4. Mrs. Johnson
   5. She
D. (Answers will vary.)
E. 1. Mary and Joan ride their bikes.
   2. Tracy has many good friends.
   3. There are lots of girls in her class.
   4. Dogs like to chew bones.
   5. My cousins are coming for a visit.
   6. We go on vacation in the summer.
   7. I wish I could cook.
   8. She bought new books.
   9. Mom gave her a cookie.
   10. I bit into the apple.
F. 1. Jordan and Jim went camping.
   2. The girls tried to find the cat.
   3. Every dollar counts.
   4. Rainbows are a sign of good luck.
   5. Did you like the candy?
   6. How are you today?
   7. Give me the ruler.
   8. Don't go there.
   9. Take it with you.
   10. Where are you going?

Progress Test 2

A. N – 1 ; 2 ; 3 ; 4 ; 5 ; 6 ; 7 ; 11 ; 12 ; 13 ; 14 ; 16
B. 1. lamp   2. sun
   3. fish   4. apple
   5. hamburger   6. cat
   7. bed   8. key
   9. snake   10. ball
   11. kite   12. dog
C. (Suggested answers)
   1. her   2. I
   3. you   4. him
   5. her   6. he
D. 1. the   2. a
   3. the   4. a
   5. an   6. the
E. 1. lives   2. touched
   3. look   4. worked

5. watched
F. 1. is working   2. learned
   3. Did ; climb   4. cooks
   5. is talking   6. can make
   7. Will ; skate   8. makes
G. 1. bright   2. old
   3. pretty   4. happy
H.

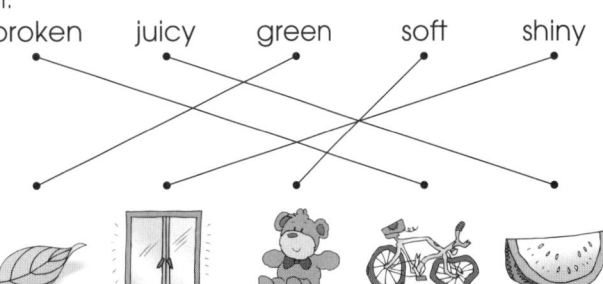

I. 1. !   2. ?   3. .
   4. .   5. ?
J. 1. The boy (took a bath).
   2. The candle (blew out).
   3. Ben (took the train).
   4. The lamp (was lit all day).
   5. Mark (is going to the doctor).
   6. The children (drew pictures on the driveway).
   7. Margaret (is visiting her aunt).
K. 1. A chicken is larger than a goat.
   2. A mouse is bigger than a house.
   3. The counter is on the knife.
   4. The floor is on the chair.
   5. A mouse can eat a snake.
   6. An apple is juicier than a strawberry.
   7. A pear is greener than a grape.
   8. The train station is higher than the CN Tower.

Section 3 Answers

1 The Five Senses

A. smell – nose ; scent ; nostrils
see – lids ; eyes ; picture
hear – ears ; loud ; sound
taste – sweet ; tongue ; sour
touch – fingers ; palm ; hard

B. 1. human 2. scent
3. hearing 4. bones
5. hand 6. hear
7. taste 8. touch

C.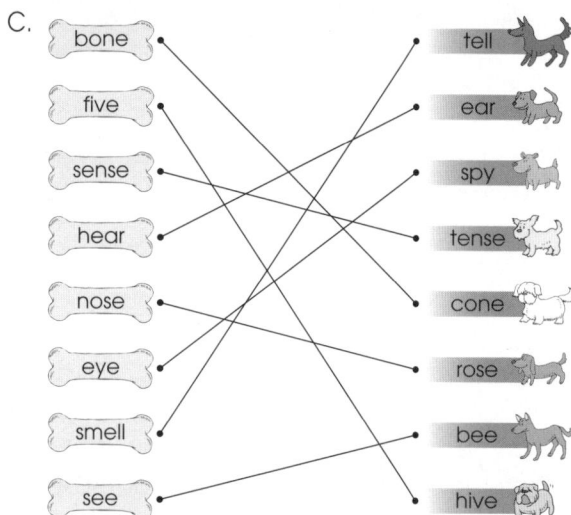

D. 1. hand 2. smell
3. taste 4. bones
5. touch 6. sense
7. eyes 8. human
9. sight 10. ears
11. nose 12. hear

E.
k	y	d	m	s	c	u	s	i	g	h	t	b	z
x	w	t	u	g	k	m	h	e	o	d	f	h	i
b	d	o	f	j	e	c	o	k	h	q	t	s	u
p	w	n	r	v	a	f	t	o	u	c	h	w	o
d	k	g	u	k	r	i	w	y	m	b	p	v	l
a	z	u	h	l	s	q	b	g	a	o	o	m	h
s	e	e	c	p	x	u	h	a	n	d	t	f	e
y	i	t	f	v	j	a	o	l	u	y	d	x	a
g	p	s	m	e	l	l	w	q	c	j	m	i	r
k	m	o	r	y	o	y	b	i	g	b	v	l	c
t	a	s	t	e	r	t	o	z	r	o	n	r	q
h	c	u	w	s	j	v	n	o	s	e	h	m	k
w	i	p	s	e	n	s	e	b	l	f	i	v	e
n	l	b	c	r	b	f	s	h	x	p	d	t	i

2 Changing Seasons

A. spring – warmer
– buds
– March
summer – August
– hot
– June
fall – orange
– yellow
– brown
winter – snow
– December
– precipitation

B.

C. (Suggested answers)
1. cud ; mud 2. dot ; got
3. bow ; low 4. bee ; see
5. down ; gown 6. pour ; tour

D. 1. four 2. fall
3. grass 4. snow
5. year 6. brown
7. season 8. warmer
9. trees

E. 1. The leaves are green.
2. Leaves are in many colours.
3. There are four seasons in every year.
4. Spring begins in March and ends in June.
5. Snow is a type of precipitation.
6. Each season is about three months long.

3 The Butterfly

A. 1. egg 2. caterpillar
   3. pupa 4. butterfly
B. 1. female 2. pupa
   3. butterfly 4. nectar
   5. colourful
C. (Suggested answers)
   1. maid ; paid 2. bat ; cat
   3. dew ; new 4. corn ; horn
   5. pale ; sale 6. hot ; pot
D. 1. egg 2. leaf
   3. caterpillar 4. pupa
   5. butterfly 6. flowers
   7. fruits
E. (Individual writing)

4 Crispy Squares

A. 1. rice 2. bowl
   3. cups 4. crispy
   5. pour 6. stove
   7. spoons 8. baking
   9. dish 10. squares
   11. saucepun 12. mixture
B. a. 1. Take the ingredients out of the fridge.
      2. Mix eggs and milk together.
      3. Pour in flour and baking powder.
      4. Pour pancake batter onto a frying pan.
   b. 1. Buy a package of balloons.
      2. Take a balloon out of the package.
      3. Blow up the balloon.
      4. Twist the opening to make a knot.
C. (Individual writing)

5 Nunavut

A. 1. territory 2. North Pole
   3. six 4. night
   5. plants 6. cold
   (7. and 8. Suggested answers)
   7. clothes 8. skidoos
B. 1. Canada 2. months
   3. cold 4. bed
   5. school 6. dark
   7. night 8. north
   9. large 10. grow
   11. plants 12. near
C. (Suggested answers)
   2. can 3. ear 4. old

5. the 6. no 7. any
8. ants 9. row 10. here
11. dark 12. day 13. light
14. out 15. side

Challenge
   (Individual answers)
D. (Individual writing)

6 Word Fun

A. (Individual answers)
B.

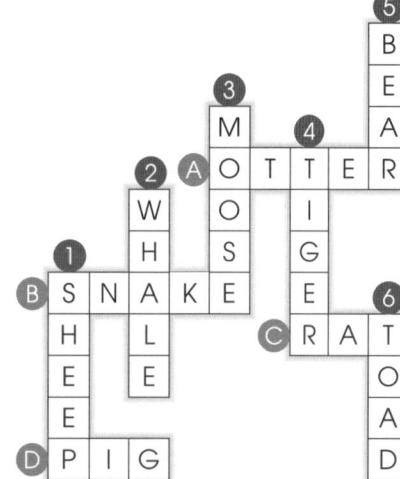

C. 1. add 2. bear 3. blue
   4. buy 5. eye 6. read
   7. flower
D. (Individual writing)
E. (Individual writing and drawing)

7 What Makes a Fish a Fish?

A. (Suggested answers)
   1. bin ; pin 2. bet ; get
   3. bill ; fill 4. bail ; fail
   5. dish ; wish 6. bake ; cake
B. 1. oseans → oceans
   2. tales → tails
   3. scails → scales
   4. waive → wave
   5. eet → eat
   6. Their → There
   7. steams → streams
   8. aguariums → aquariums
C. 1. Fish live in ponds and oceans.
   2. Fish swim by moving their tails.
   3. All fish have backbones.
   4. Gills help fish to breathe.
   5. Scales protect the fish's skin.

Section 3 Answers

   6. Some fish make good pets.
D. (Individual writing)

Challenge
   (Individual writing)

Progress Test 1

A. 1. box 2. cup
   3. sock 4. bat
   5. cake 6. milk
   7. goose 8. palm
   9. leaf 10. scales
   11. insect 12. gill
B. (Suggested answers)
   2. top 3. pot
   4. art 5. ear
   6. eat 7. wit
   8. son 9. sum
   10. old 11. and
   12. is 13. ray
   14. sea 15. our
   16. cook 17. war
   18. plan
C. 1. Mike plays with his computer.
   2. Amanda swims in her pool.
   3. There are four books on the table.
   4. The sun is hot today.
   5. Caitlin has a pair of red shoes.
   6. Bats look for food in the dark.
D. 1. skates 2. paints
   3. driving 4. riding
   5. plays 6. licking
   7. watered 8. sucking
   9. cut 10. danced
E. 1. sale → sail
   2. plaid → played
   3. maid → made
   4. trayed → trade
   5. eight → ate
   6. male → mail
   7. two → too
   8. flour → flower
F. (Suggested answers)
   1. maid ; paid ; raid 2. dot ; got ; jot
   3. hour ; pour ; sour 4. pale ; sale ; tale
   5. cap ; gap ; map 6. bin ; pin ; sin
   7. bet ; get ; let 8. ball ; fall ; tall
   9. bill ; fill ; hill 10. bake ; cake ; fake
   11. fail ; jail ; sail 12. dear ; fear ; gear

8 Bat Facts

A. (Suggested answers)
   1. bats 2. country
   3. world 4. places
   5. fruits 6. insects
B.
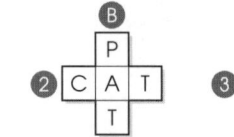 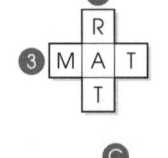

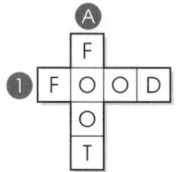 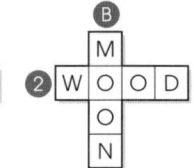 

C. (Individual writing)
D. (Individual writing)

9 The Emperor Penguin

A. 1. penguin 2. Emperor
   3. Antarctic 4. krill
   5. hatches 6. patches
   7. black 8. yellow
   9. taller 10. grey / goes
B. 1. largest 2. penguin
   3. feathers 4. ocean
   5. shrimp 6. father
C. 1. The Emperor Penguin lives in Antarctica.
   2. It lives near water, never on dry land.
   3. Penguins get their food from the ocean.
   4. Fish and krill are food for penguins.
   5. The Emperor is the largest of penguins.
   6. The mother penguin hunts for food.
   7. The father Emperor hatches the egg.
D. 1. I love all kinds of candies. ~~Fish is not my favourite food.~~ My favourite candies are gummy bears.
   2. I have a new bike. It is red and white. ~~The car goes in the garage.~~ My bike stays in the storage shed.
   3. Amanda loves to swim in her pool. She asks her friends to come for a swim. ~~The flowers grow tall.~~ Her friends like to swim too.
   4. Some of the best T.V. shows I like are really funny. They make me laugh and laugh. ~~My mom likes to dance.~~

10 Playing Soccer

A. (Individual writing)

B.
Column A	Column B
1. tall	ladybug
2. green	ball
3. tiny	knife
4. blue	girl
5. round	tree
6. sharp	grass
7. pretty	candy
8. sweet	sky
9. rainy	game
10. fun	day

(Matches: 1-girl, 2-grass, 3-ladybug, 4-sky, 5-ball, 6-knife, 7-candy, 8-tree, 9-day, 10-game — as drawn)

C. (Colour the words.)
1. tiny
2. huge
3. twice
4. tall
5. a few
6. robbers
7. fast

D. 1. soccer
2. field
3. children
4. age
5. uniforms
6. coach
7. friendly
8. practise
9. games
10. fun

Challenge
(Individual writing)

11 Ladybugs

A. (Suggested answers)
1. best
2. hot
3. dug
4. hat
5. back
6. give
7. bill
8. come

B. 1. a bug that is red and black
2. an insect that eats plants and is eaten by ladybugs
3. They eat the inside of ladybugs.
4. someone or something that kills ladybugs
5. a spray to kill insects
6. a place where birds live
7. mess up
8. low green bushes
9. a bright colour
10. dots

C. 1. ladybug
2. insect
3. summer
4. useful
5. winter
6. disturb
7. because
8. lifetime

D. 1. Ladybugs are black and red. / Ladybugs are red and black.
2. They live in flowers and shrubs. / They live in shrubs and flowers.
3. They live in trees and houses in winter. / They live in houses and trees in winter.
4. Ladybugs are useful because they eat insects.
5. Ladybugs are insects that eat aphides.
6. Ladybugs have some enemies.
7. Human beings are also the enemies of ladybugs.

12 The New Umbrella

A. (Suggested answers)
1. yell
2. hen
3. so
4. in
5. hat
6. old
7. sun
8. eat
9. ears
10. out
11. or
12. as

B. (word search grid with: umbrella, modern, handle, really, protect, rain, neat, twirl, etc.)

C. 1. My new umbrella is colourful. / My colourful umbrella is new.
2. My umbrella is not too big.
3. It is fun to twirl the umbrella.
4. The first umbrella was used in Egypt.
5. The umbrella protects me from the sun.
6. Umbrellas were used in Scotland in the 1800's.
7. I use my umbrellas in the rain.

D. 1. My mom bought me an umbrella. It was a present for my seventh birthday. It is red, blue, and yellow. It looks really neat. ~~My mom made me a huge birthday cake.~~
2. I have a new umbrella. It is colourful. ~~It was cloudy yesterday.~~ I can use it in the rain and also in the sun.

Complete EnglishSmart • Grade 2

Section 3 Answers

3. My neighbour, Jenny, has an umbrella hat. It is an umbrella but it is also a hat. She wears it on her head. ~~We often play together after school.~~ She looks cute in her umbrella hat.

E. (Individual drawing and writing)

13 Sam the Firefighter

A. 1. firefighter 2. works
   3. station 4. equipment
   5. friends 6. duty
   7. hours 8. hoses
   9. house 10. clean
   11. sometimes 12. overnight

B. 1. There were lots of bluejays in the garden. They were eating seeds and sitting on tree branches. ~~We had lunch there.~~
   2. Sunflowers can grow almost as tall as a one-storey house. ~~The apple is tasty.~~ Even the sunflower seeds are pretty big.
   3. William has a new red bike. He can ride it without training wheels. ~~His sister has a toothache.~~
   4. Jane liked the flowers. ~~She went to school.~~ She picked some flowers for her dad.
   5. Vincent ran all the way to the park. He played on the monkey bars. ~~William went shopping with his mom.~~
   6. There are seven days in every week. Sunday is the first day of the week. ~~I enjoyed the show.~~ Saturday is the last day.
   7. Our car was dirty. We went to the carwash yesterday. ~~There are little flies in the bushes.~~ Now the car is clean and shiny.

C. 1. eight 2. bare
   3. buy 4. sense
   5. wait 6. sum
   7. here 8. new
   9. flour 10. cell
   11. be 12. court

D. (Individual writing)

14 The Cactus

A. (Individual writing)
B. 1. dessert → desert
   2. shellow → shallow
   3. cactas → cactus
   4. peried → period
   5. expend → expand
   6. stord → stored
   7. think → thick
   8. ranefall → rainfall

C. 1. hot → cold
   2. much → little
   3. short → long
   4. slowly → quickly
   5. thin → thick
   6. shrink → expand
   7. thick → shallow

D. (Individual writing)

15 Marineland

A. 1. Marineland is in Niagara Falls, Canada.
   2. There are sea animals there.
   3. There is so much fun in Marineland.
   4. Roller-coaster rides are very exciting.

B.
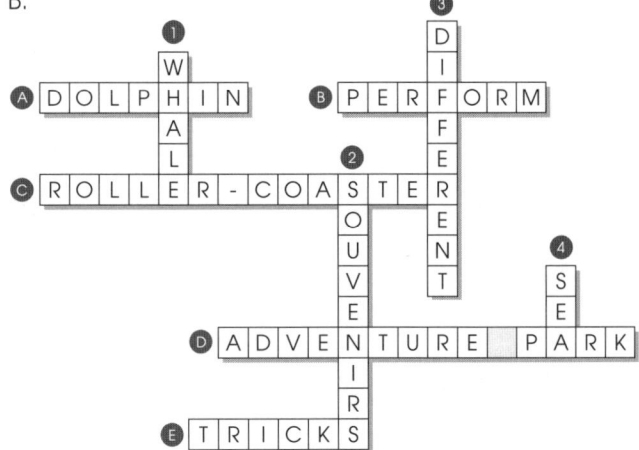

C. 1. Moon 2. Apple
   3. Red 4. I
   5. Nest 6. Easy
   7. Ladybug 8. Ant
   9. Night 10. Dog
   MARINELAND

D. (Individual writing)
Challenge
   (Individual drawing and writing)

Progress Test 2

A. 1. doll 2. books
   3. bike 4. cat
   5. dog 6. popsicles
   7. pillow 8. house

9. clown
11. bed
13. glass
15. tree
17. girl
19. street
21. day
23. road

10. plant
12. car
14. light
16. cap
18. firefighter
20. box
22. breakfast
24. whale

F. 1. trane → train
2. peeple → people
3. fiends → friends
4. seads → seeds
5. advanture → adventure
6. friut → fruit
7. petting → patting
8. glass → grass
9. Penguins → Penguins
10. feeld → field

B.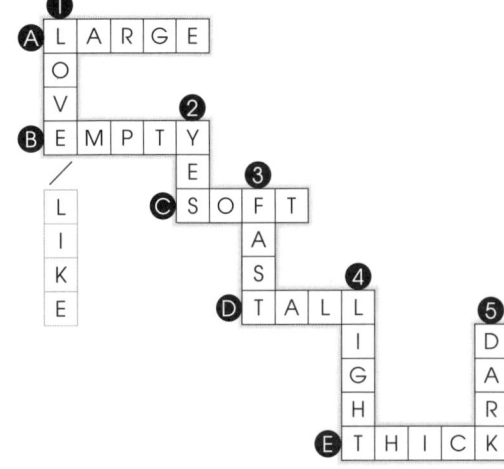

C. 1. My favourite candies are jujubes. / Jujubes are my favourite candies.
2. Judy is my sister's good friend. / My sister's good friend is Judy.
3. Ice cream is so good in summer.
4. Many people visit Toronto Zoo.
5. I like to go swimming.
6. We read a lot of books.
7. Firefighters work for many hours.
8. Dolphins are clever sea animals.

D. 1. large
3. quickly
5. smart
7. much

2. small
4. one time
6. pretty
8. kind

E. (Suggested answers)
1. best
3. pick
5. new
7. beat
9. pour
11. whale
13. late
15. drop
17. dare
19. gill
21. mug
23. full

2. up
4. bead
6. stay
8. deal
10. brain
12. turn
14. hand
16. never
18. treat
20. aid
22. live
24. sold

1. 1. clock 2. glue
   3. black 4. sled
   5. plus 6. flag

2.

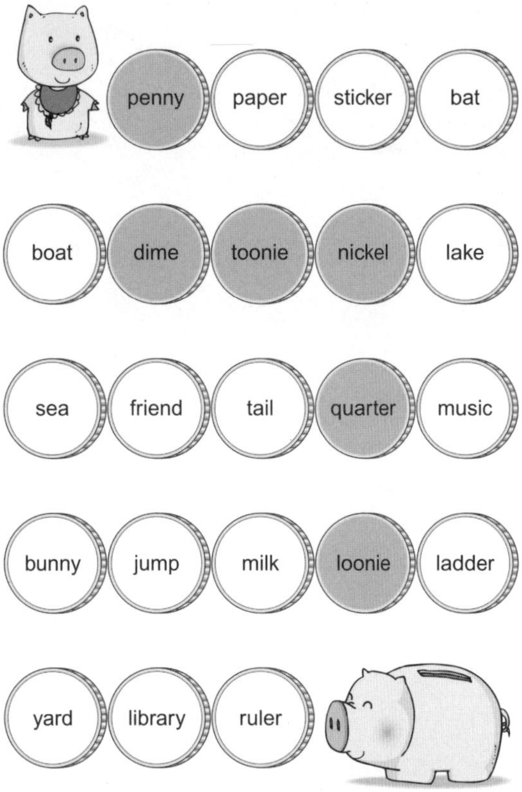

3.

s	b	l	i	f	e	b	e	l	t
u	a	q	c	k	v	s	o	p	o
n	m	n	s	g	d	u	e	a	w
g	p	b	d	o	j	n	w	i	e
l	m	h	r	c	s	h	e	l	l
a	k	c	t	e	a	w	a	z	s
s	a	n	d	o	l	s	j	t	p
s	e	a	g	u	l	l	t	y	a
e	x	r	l	e	n	v	a	l	d
s	w	i	m	s	u	i	t	e	e

4. 1. radio 2. dolphin
   3. fish 4. pen
   5. second

5. (Suggested answers)
   1. son 2. far
   3. ape 4. bed
   5. pal 6. hose

6.

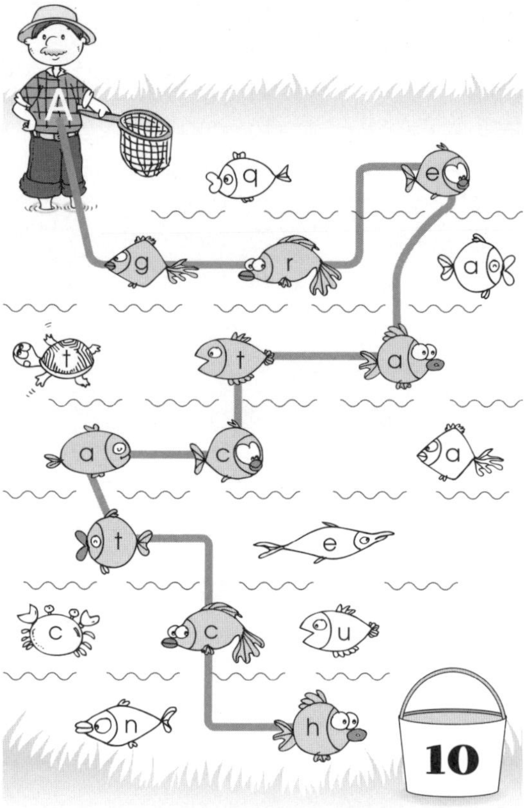

7.

1 M	O	U	S	2 E			3 F		
I				G		4 B	I	R	5 D
L		6 P	I	G			S		O
7 K	8 R			S			H		G
	A								
	9 B	U	10 N	N	Y			11 C	
	B		O					A	
	I		S		12 W	I	N	G	S
	13 T	O	E	S				E	

8. 1. fawn 2. puppy
   3. duckling 4. cub
   5. piglet 6. calf

9.

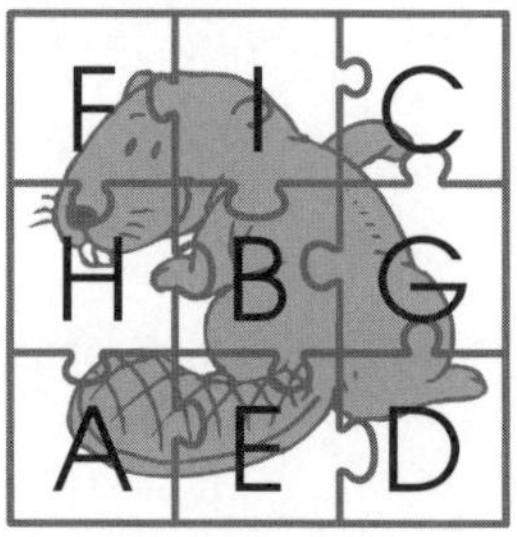

beaver

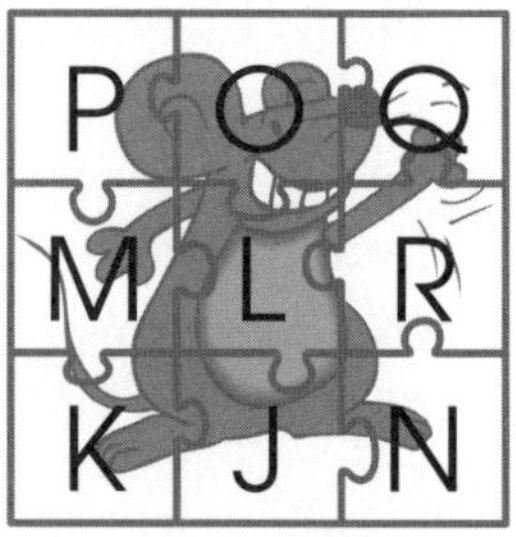

rat / mouse

10.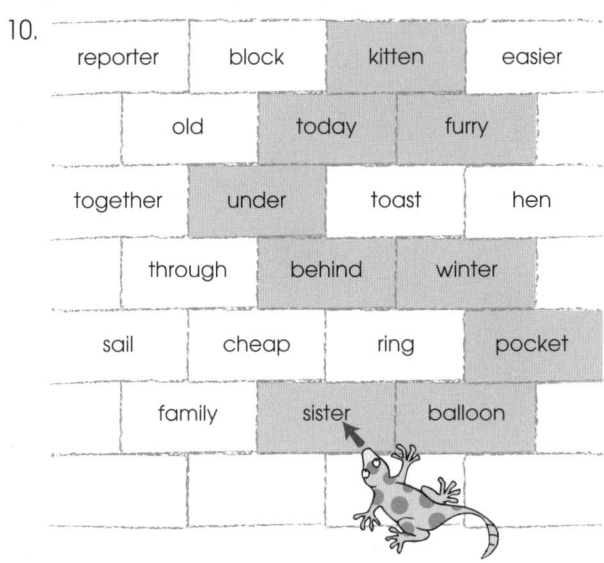

11. ink – pink ; dot – spot ; talk – walk ; boat – float ;
    cake – bake ; swim – dim

12.
c	m	g	o	s	p	r	a	c	x	a	p
g	h	o	r	s	e	a	f	o	t	c	i
k	d	t	a	h	o	d	u	p	e	l	e
n	y	x	b	k	c	o	w	i	t	o	s
s	a	u	b	c	t	g	o	g	a	q	h
o	e	d	i	g	o	o	s	e	b	a	e
d	t	u	t	p	a	r	a	o	b	t	e
v	m	c	h	i	c	k	e	n	i	b	p
g	c	k	d	g	d	s	m	h	f	w	r
o	r	c	n	v	p	z	e	z	q	x	n
a	j	u	o	a	x	g	b	y	u	d	w
t	u	r	k	e	y	c	s	b	v	t	k

13. t r a s u n ☾ ◇ ☾
    e r d e w t △ ♡ △
    a s i n t   ☆ ○ ☆
    b c h n t   Ⓢ ♡ Ⓢ

    ☆ ○ ☆

14. 1. Monkey   2. Giraffe
    3. Gorilla   4. Elephant
    5. Panda   6. Lion

15.
¹O	²N	E		³W	A	S	P	⁵S	
	E			N				T	
⁶M	O	S	Q	U	I	T	O		
O		T		S				N	
T						⁷P		G	
H		⁸C	R	I	C	K	E	T	S
		R				S			
		A		⁹B	E	E	T	L	¹⁰E
		W		E		S			G
¹¹F	L	I	E	S					G

16.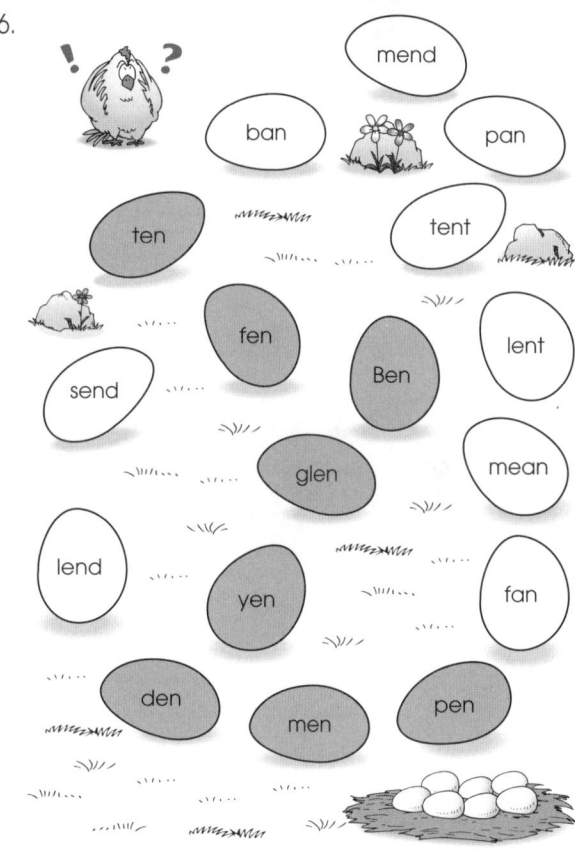

Section 4 Answers

17.

18. (Individual colouring)

19. My naughty dog hides his favourite bones under my bed.

20.

	¹W	²A	T	E	R	M	E	L	³O	N
		P							R	
		⁴P	E	A	⁵R		⁶E	A	T	
		L			I		N			
		E			P		G			
				⁷P	E	E	L			
				E			⁸S			
				⁹A	P	R	I	C	O	T
				C				U		
				H				¹⁰R	E	D